WHAT THE PREACHER FORGOT TO TELL ME

IDENTITY AND GOSPEL IN JAMAICA

what the

Preacher

forgot to *Tell* me

Identity and Gospel in Jamaica
by Faith Linton

BayRidge
B O O K S

an imprint of Castle Quay Books Canada

What the Preacher Forgot to Tell Me: Identity and Gospel in Jamaica

Copyright ©2009 Faith Elaine Linton
Printed in Canada
International Standard Book Number: 978-1-897213-36-0

Published by:
BayRidge Books: an imprint of Castle Quay Books Canada
1-1295 Wharf Street, Pickering, Ontario, L1W 1A2
Tel: (416) 573-3249
E-mail: lwillard@castlequaybooks.com
www.castlequaybooks.com

Written by Faith Linton
Copy editing by Marina H. Hofman
Printed at Essence Printing, Belleville, Ontario

Library and Archives Canada Cataloguing in Publication

Linton, Faith, 1949-

What the preacher forgot to tell me : identity and gospel in Jamaica / Faith Linton ; editor: Marina H. Hofman.

ISBN 978-1-897213-36-0

1. Preaching--Jamaica. 2. Preaching--Caribbean Area. 3. Linton, Faith, 1949-. 4. God--Biblical teaching. 5. Identification (Religion). I. Hofman, Marina H. II. Title.

BR645.J3L55 2008   251.0097292   C2008-906774-6

BayRidge
B O O K S

To my husband, Ivan,
patient, gracious,
solidly supportive

TABLE OF CONTENTS

TABLE OF CONTENTS

ACKNOWLEDGEMENTS

I WANT TO THANK DR. ANTHONY ALLEN, FORMER MEMBER OF THE BOARD of Governors of the United Theological College of the West Indies, who put into my mind the idea of writing this book. He listened to my twenty-minute presentation on Alienation, Identity and the Preaching of the Gospel, and said to me afterwards: "You have to develop this topic."

My main support and encouragement, and my most trenchant critics, during the writing process, have been my twin sister and her husband, Joyce and Graham Gladwell. I have benefited enormously from their writing and editing skills, and I thank them more than I can express.

I acknowledge with deep gratitude the willingness of the following contributors to tell their stories: Maria Davis, Lucy deCarteret, Trevor and Elizabeth Thomas-Hope and Michelle Sampeur.

I thank YWAM Publishing and the authors John Dekker and Lois Neely for their permission to quote extensively from the book *Torches of Joy,* which provides remarkable supportive evidence for the main theme of this work.

I am particularly grateful to Castle Quay Books, the publisher, Larry Willard, and his editorial assistant, Marina H. Hofman. In addition to providing professional services, they have shown insightful appreciation of the heart of this work.

I record with pleasure the help of my friend, Dahlia Fraser. She is the person I have relied on most to move the publication from copy to printed product. For putting at my disposal her specialist skills in editing and publishing, for her keen personal interest and the networking by which she brought together the key persons in this project, I owe her an incalculable debt of gratitude.

Very special thanks are due to my personal assistant and friend, Jacqueline Watson. Her patience and cheerful willingness, together with her computer skills, have made the day-to-day task seem light and easy.

With thankfulness in my heart above all to God, I send this book on its way with the hope and prayer that God's Holy Spirit will use it to bring enlightenment and transformation to each reader.

FOREWORD

FAITH LINTON IS A TEACHER OF TEACHERS. HER REMARKABLE TEACHING GIFT has been shaped by over 40 years of experience in classrooms, conferences, and retreats centers in Jamaica and across the Caribbean. In these settings, she has listened, counseled, and engaged with young people growing up in the swift changing cultural currents of Caribbean societies. She has witnessed first-hand the problem of negative self-descriptions and negative self-identities which characterize so many of our young people.

Encountering this problem for so many years in so many places in the Caribbean, Faith Linton has developed a deep concern. This concern is for the restoration of the dignity of personhood in Caribbean societies. Psychologists, social workers, and educators, among others, have been wrestling with manifestations of this problem in the form of distorted identities and deep behavioural problems of today's young people. While the loss of dignity of personhood in the Caribbean is very much a part of the scars of its history, misguided parenting, poor social living conditions, and misguided preaching of the gospel often reinforce it. These are factors that condition and shape values and attitudes. With religion being such a dominant factor in Caribbean culture, the overwhelming impact of the preaching of the gospel on people's self-understanding is yet to be properly assessed.

In this book, Faith Linton tells the stories of some of the young people she's met. Their stories reflect the pain and struggle of a generation of young Caribbeans emerging into adulthood, seeking to find real identity and meaning in life. The fact that their pain and struggle somehow mirror the pain and struggle of their societies that are emerging out of stages of under-development and into the modernity of developing states is of little comfort. It's a difficult rite of passage. The struggle takes many forms and manifests itself in many ways, some-times in very negative terms.

But this book goes beyond story-telling. It offers a constructive way out of the pervasive, corroding, and ultimately self-destructive notions of some forms of Caribbean identity. The way out, the author argues, is based on grasping the significance of the original design of the creation story in first chapter of the Book of Genesis. Her use of the creation narrative in Genesis chapter 1 has helped many young people experience new and healthy visions of themselves as human beings, made in the image and likeness of God, the Creator. Affirming this understanding of the truth of the biblical story of creation has important implications, especially for preachers of the gospel. When young people begin to grasp the significance of this, they begin to see that they are therefore people of God-given dignity and self-worth. This is good news. It is as if the light is turned on. Their self-understanding and self-esteem begin to take on healthy and constructive meaning.

The real lesson of the stories shared in this book is something that needs to be grasped by all who help to teach and nurture the young generation. Preaching the right gospel has implications not only for people's eternal salvation but also for their earthly salvation. Faith Linton writes with great skill and insight. She teaches those who teach others, and that means most of us. This is a book that should be read and re-read over and over again.

Las G. Newman
President,
Caribbean Graduate School of Theology

PROLOGUE

MEDITATION ON GENESIS 1 AND 2

UNDERSTANDING GENESIS 1 AND 2 IS THE KEY FOR GRASPING THE TRUTHS OF this book and the basis for a right understanding of our identity.

IN THE BEGINNING, GOD CREATED EVERYTHING

This is the truth that lays the foundation for my relationship with God and understanding of myself.

God is the source of my life. Every aspect and detail of my being—physical, mental, emotional, and spiritual—was designed and fashioned by Him.

I acknowledge my complete dependence on Him.

I recognize the claim that He, the Creator, has on my life.

I acknowledge His supreme authority, His perfect knowledge, absolute power, and sovereign control over all He has made.

GOD HAS REVEALED HIMSELF AS PERSONAL, WARM, INVOLVED, AND CARING

He is not a cold, impassive entity, ordering all things with detached self-sufficiency.

His name is Love.

His character is good, upright. He is utterly trustworthy.

This is the God who created me.

I AM MADE IN HIS IMAGE

I am the pinnacle of God's creation, the highest of all the forms of life that He has made.

I am in a special category, distinct from every other, for He designed me to be like Him in essence and in character.

Essence: At the very heart of my being, I am spiritual, capable of knowing the God who is Spirit, capable of a close, personal relationship with my Creator.

Character: I am made for goodness. I am meant to be morally pure and upright, utterly trustworthy, warm, involved and caring, full of love towards God, my fellow-creatures, and myself.

THERE IS A PURPOSE FOR MY LIFE

"Let us," said God, "make man in our image, in our likeness, and *let them rule* over the fish of the sea and the birds of the air, over the livestock, over all the earth, and over all the creatures that move along the ground" (Genesis 1:26, author's emphasis).

This awesome power and responsibility, delegated to us by the Creator, demonstrates, even in its misuse, the significance of humankind.

I AM MADE FOR RELATIONSHIP

So God created man in his
own image,
In the image of God he
created him,
Male and female he created
them. (Genesis 1:27)

"It is not good for the man to be alone" (Genesis 2:18). It is not good because man is the image of God and God is not alone. God is love. Within Himself He lives in relationship as Father, Son, and Spirit.

So we too are made for relationship.

The first human relationship God created was between the man and woman.

Together they rule over the earth (Genesis 1:26).

Together they bring into being new unique expressions of God's likeness (Genesis 1:28).

Together they represent the complete image of God (Genesis 1:27).

A world made up of the one without the other would be forever lacking, for the revelation of God's image would be incomplete.

WE NEED REDEMPTION

God gave the man and the woman the privilege of choice.

We made the wrong choice.

Sin entered in.

Sin has permeated our lives.

We are in need of redemption.

Redemption offers us a rescue and a restoration—a rescue from the forces of darkness in whose power we find ourselves, and a restoration to the goodness and love in which we were created.

In light of these great truths, why do I find myself telling everybody about sin, which came later, and neglecting to mention the beauty and goodness in which God first conceived me?

Karen was one who needed to hear about the original "beauty" and "goodness" of humanity. It illustrates the tragedy of wrong choices. It points to our incredible destiny in Christ and the unique place that all God's people have in His glorious plan for the universe. In particular, it illustrates the importance of understanding the truths of Genesis 1 and 2. It was when Karen grasped these truths that she experienced the transforming power of knowing who we are in God's eyes.

We Need Redemption

God gave the man and the woman the privilege of choice.
We made the wrong choice.
Sin entered in.
Sin has separated us from...
We are in need of redemption.

ONE

KAREN'S STORY

ALIENATION TO IDENTIFICATION

THE TRAUMA OF ALIENATION BEGAN FOR KAREN, WHILE SHE WAS STILL IN THE womb. Here she tells the moving story of her wounded life:

"I was born in Brooklyn, New York, 1971. My birth was a miracle. My mother rejected me as soon as she knew she was pregnant. She'd decided to have an abortion when a friend of the family pleaded with her: 'Don't abort that baby! God gave it to you for a reason.' So God intervened and rescued me.

"Needless to say, I did not receive a warm welcome at birth. For the second time, God intervened. He put it in the hearts of my great uncle and aunt to come forward and ask if they could raise me. They took me in and brought me up as their own. My mother provided financially and visited me occasionally on weekends.

"Throughout my life there were times when my mother wanted to parent me, and she'd try. Occasionally we'd be together for months at a time. Also there were times I'd be living with my grandmother or other family members for short periods. All this passing around made me feel quite disoriented and unattached—yet I learned to survive.

"I remember my father as my knight in shining armour! We had amazing adventures together. I remember trips upstate to Woodstock, camping on cliffs in the parks, tasting my first tongue sandwich, and eating homemade marble cake on that amazing cliff overlooking the water. I remember nude sunbathers, the Rainbow Shop, red sports cars, and his attractive girlfriends. One even took the time to explain the numeric markings on her forearm, tattooed while she was in a concentration camp.

17

"Life was good whenever I saw or thought of my father. He really loved me, and it made me feel on top of the world. Unfortunately our times together were few and far between.

"I missed being mothered as well. I remember the hopeless sense of abandonment, the never-ending clawing in me to be found, acknowledged, wanted, treasured, and desired. My mother and I were spending more and more weekends together, but they were painful.

"My mother made fun of me in front of family members, teasing me about my large nose, for example. She hounded me for every little thing. It seemed that she could only see what was wrong with me. Nothing I did was good enough. No report card satisfied her, even though in my early years at school I never failed to make the honor roll. I was pouring out my love on a woman who could never seem to love me in return, and it hurt more than I can tell.

"As I grew older I began to understand my mother better. She'd had a tough life. Deprived of both father and mother, she felt unlovable and ill-equipped to love and care for a child of her own. As a result, I, in turn, grew up feeling unlovable.

"Perhaps the most unselfish and sacrificial thing my mother ever did was to give me to my great aunt and uncle to raise. They provided me with a stable and disciplined life, enriched by the educational and cultural opportunities for which New York is famous. But, in spite of all that, every day was a reminder that I was at one place because I wasn't wanted someplace else.

"I was a deeply unhappy child. I felt unworthy, unloved, unlovable, rejected, and inferior. There was an abiding rage and anger inside me. I suffered mood swings and became more and more emotionally unstable. I was attracted to the morbid and the depressing and came close to suicide at times. It seemed that everyone and everything had failed to meet my need for connectedness and intimacy.

"By the age of 16 I was determined to be loved, determined that if all I had was physical attraction, then I would make someone love me at last. I already knew, well before then, how attractive I was to the opposite sex. I had learned to seduce at an early age. All I really wanted was to be loved and accepted. It would be many years before I received the answer to this desperate cry.

"In my senior year, I met a young man in night school. I was taking courses to make up for my poor performance during the year. This young man came with his own package of pain, brokenness, and darkness. When I told him my own life story he promised to be both father and mother to me. I knew all along that he never could, but he wanted to try, so I let him. We spent the next four years self-destructing together.

"Then God intervened. This was His supreme intervention in my life, one that turned me from the path of absolute darkness to absolute light.

"It happened when I was 21.

"I had left my adoptive home several years before, had traveled all over the city adopting various families, and had finally landed up at the home of one of my best friends from high school. We were both seeking, broken and lost. My religion was a self-made cocktail of Zen Buddhism, New Age, Islam, Ancestral Worship, much edited Christianity, and Rastafarianism, topped off with a strong dose of human secularism. I had grown gorgeous dreadlocks by this time and in my inner circle of friends changed my name to mean "Mother Earth." I smoked marijuana constantly. My friend and I saw ourselves as "naturalists," claiming (ironically) that we didn't want to put chemicals in our systems, even while we were destroying ourselves in other ways.

"One day we were sitting together in her room, smoking and eating and listening to a gospel song by a group we loved. The words went something like this:

Holy Lord, my perfect peace,
Please let this pain and sorrow cease.
I know with you by my side
Love and hope will rise.
All glory, hallelujah,
We praise Your holy name.
I yield, I yield
To You, Lord,
Please take my hand.

"As these words rang out, the atmosphere in the room changed. My friend, sensing what was happening, turned to me and without a word removed the plate of food from my lap. I fell face forward, crawling

19

and weeping as the Spirit of God confronted me through every note and word. I felt God's Spirit sing prayers to the Father through me, using a song I'd listened to many times before.

"In that moment I became aware of the presence of God enveloping me in the most personal and tangible way.

"A few weeks later I was invited to attend a church service. It was at that service I publicly professed what had already transpired in my heart and life. I went forward and asked the Lord Jesus Christ to come into my heart, not realizing that He had already done so.

"I continued to attend that church and requested baptism, not just once, but three times. Not understanding the radical, powerful, and complete work that God had done in my life, I felt that I could not be clean after just one baptism. I still believed that deep inside, I was the same unclean, unworthy, hopeless soul that had to grovel to receive a little of the love, affection, attention, and forgiveness of the Lord. I did not yet understand that I was already His, fully forgiven, completely clean in His sight, that Jesus had come and taken up residence within me, and He would never leave me.

"Then something happened that demonstrated beyond all doubt that a radical change had indeed taken place in me. Not long after my conversion, my ex-boyfriend appeared in my life again. He wanted us to get together and talk. I agreed to see him. One thing led to another and we ended up, as usual, in bed. This time however, I immediately became frightened, sick to my stomach, and overwhelmed with grief. I felt as if the heavens had rolled away and God Himself was looking right at me and had caught me in a gigantic landfill of sewage and foul garbage. All the depravity and degradation of that four-year period while I lived with my boyfriend rose up to confront me. Quickly I grabbed my clothing, got dressed, and ran out of the house in tears. Heartbroken and in pain, I rode home, in full conviction of sin.

"Once I reached my house, I ran past my best friend straight into the bathroom and fell over the toilet bowl in gut-wrenching tears to the Father. I begged Him to forgive me. I was so distraught that the greater miracle escaped me at the time. I did not recognize that here was proof that I had been changed indeed.

"A few weeks later when friends offered me a smoke, I found myself sincerely and peacefully responding, 'No, thank you.' I sat there on the house stoop as my friends smoked, silently glowing as the truth came home to me that I really didn't want to smoke anymore. I was engulfed by the gentle, peaceful Presence who held me in contentment and grace.

"The following year was one of such intimacy and love from the Lord that I cannot express it. How He called me! How He drew me! Even now His work of deliverance, healing, and restoration continues in me day after day. Though still imperfect, I am growing up in God, increasingly secure in a love that is greater than my young heart knew how to ask for, and greater than my adult heart can fathom. I have a Mother, Father, Friend, Husband, Lover, Master, Redeemer, Saviour, Answer, Listener, Guide, Counselor and Life.

"In 1998 I journeyed to St. Croix to attend a Youth With A Mission (YWAM) Discipleship Training School (DTS).

"I came to St. Croix hungry to know more about God. As I read Psalm 8 during my personal devotions, the psalmist's question in verse 4 caught my attention: 'What is man, that thou art mindful of him?' (KJV). The question stuck in my mind: 'What is man?' I found myself pondering, searching, putting the question to God.

"A few weeks later, to my amazement, one of the teachers spoke on the biblical answer to the question: Who am I? My eyes were opened to the remarkable picture found in Genesis 1 and 2 of the dignity, beauty and wonder of man and woman, as God originally designed them.

"All the theology and Bible teaching I had been exposed to made sense when I realized how valuable each person is to God. We are valuable because of what God invested in us when He made us in His image, the pinnacle of His creation, His masterpiece. The gospel message made sense in a new way. Genesis 1 and 2 laid the foundation for the message, giving the rationale for all the rest of our spiritual history. Our value in God's eyes was the key.

"This insight revolutionized my thinking about myself and my life as a Christian. God had already revealed Himself to me as my Saviour and the source of all I longed for from mother, father, friend, lover, guide, and counselor. I knew to whom I belonged, and that knowledge had healed the deep-rooted sense of alienation I had lived with all of my life. But I still struggled with a sense of unworthiness. Like the Psalmist, I wondered what God saw in me. But now in Genesis 1 and 2

I found my identity in God's eyes. The discovery inevitably transformed my approach to evangelism.

"Shortly after this, the time came for us YWAM students to outreach to the hurting and needy, putting into practice all we had been learning in our DTS. Before we left, the DTS coordinator summed up the approach we should take in sharing the gospel: 'Tell them that each of them is a damaged masterpiece in need of restoration.' We followed his advice, in at least one case with dramatic effect.

"My YWAM student team visited Brazil. One evening we put on a program for a group of about 40 night school students ages 15 to 40 years. They were a tough bunch, including pregnant teenage girls, angry young boys, hostile men, and women bitter from so many bad choices and situations. These were the alienated. Society had given up on them. They were 'nobodies.'

"The school had previously tried to hold evangelistic meetings for this group, with terrible results. The students would boo the speakers, throw things, or walk out.

"Before going to the school that evening, we spent time in prayer. However, the evening began in chaos. The music wasn't working properly, the sound system was in and out of commission, the kids were restless, and we were nervous! It seemed that our worst fears were about to materialize. Soon the restless students would start to act up or walk out. Instead, there was an amazing turnaround. By the time the dramas began, the students were all seated and watching everything with perfect attention. The cigarettes were put out and all eyes were forward. There was no doubt in our minds that the Holy Spirit had stepped in.

"The time came to share the message of the gospel. What would they hear? A message that confirmed their sense of hopelessness and despair? No. One that convinced them of their utter depravity and worthlessness and implied that this was all that God saw in them? No. One that provided no rationale for His love so that His death on the cross seemed a wasted sacrifice? No. This time, it was different. Yes, they were sinners, no denying that, but not one of them was a loser, not one was hopeless in God's eyes. No wrong choice on their part could change how much God valued them.

"In other words, the team shared not from the angle of Hell and damnation but from the truth of each person's value in God's eyes.

"It was amazing to see with my own eyes the face of a hardened young woman in the front row soften as she heard not only with her ears but also with her heart that she was somebody very special. Tears began to well up in her eyes as she discovered that she mattered to God. Her tears were only one drop of many that fell that night as we were all overwhelmed by the love and presence of Jesus Christ. You could feel God's Spirit opening hearts and entering in. Many people came to genuinely know Jesus that night."

JAMAICA NEEDS THIS TOO

What Karen and her team witnessed that evening in the Brazilian school is the breakthrough that so many Christians are praying for. They are praying for this for their community, their society, their nation. As I reflect on the situation in my own country, Jamaica, I see that many are alienated and without a sense of identity in spite of decades of Christian teaching. My prayer is: "Would to God that this breakthrough could be repeated, multiplied, in every district, village, town, and city in my own country."

CAN THE CHURCH MAKE A DIFFERENCE?

MY HOMELAND, JAMAICA, FEATURES IN THE *GUINNESS BOOK OF RECORDS* AS having more churches per square mile than any other country in the world. We seem set to break another world record, that of being the country with the greatest number of evangelistic crusades per year, per person.

During the last 350 years of our history, Christianity has remained the dominant religion, and it has flourished numerically in the last 50 years. The role of the church in the development of our society has been well documented. Beginning in the latter part of the 18th century, Christian missionaries not only preached to our enslaved African ancestors, they were also actively engaged in the spiritual and political battle for the abolition of slavery.

When the slaves were finally set free in 1838, these missionaries were the ones mainly responsible for setting up villages where they guided these newly freed people in organizing their lives as families and communities.

One outstanding contribution of the church at this time was education. The church provided schools for those who for generations had been illiterate. Thus, the church brought spiritual light and hope; it led the way to moral transformation and a release of the creative and productive powers of our people. This work continues today.

At the same time, we face a puzzling and disturbing situation. Side by side with the remarkable success of the gospel, there has been a marked rise in the rate of crime and violence, particularly in the last 30 years. According to the statistics, we are ranked among the four or five most violent societies in the world. Sexually transmitted diseases are endemic—regularly found in the population. Family life is at an all-time low, with more than 80 percent of all children being born out of wedlock and a large proportion of that number growing up without a father's presence or care.

We do have bright and gifted Jamaicans who are well qualified to take up key positions in politics, the church, public and private sectors, finance, industry, and commerce. However, we are shocked and disappointed at how frequently we hear reports of corrupt practices on the part of some of these leaders.

The question is this: How can we explain the seeming failure of the church's presentation of the gospel to permeate the whole society with Christian values, raising the moral standards and quality of life in this gospel-saturated country? The history of Christianity testifies over and over that the gospel has this power. For example, in the 18th century, following the preaching of John Wesley, British society was transformed. The effects of this transformation lasted for generations. Why has this not happened in Jamaica?

There is no simple answer to this question. A variety of factors are involved. However, when we look at our history, we can understand something of the nature and complexity of our moral dilemma. The history of today's Caribbean nations began in slavery, a condition that lasted almost 400 years. Our major problems are, in large part, the legacy of slavery and the plantation system.

The brutal removal of our African ancestors from their homeland resulted in the "severing of those forms of human relationship that were most precious to the African: the ties with family, kinfolk, tribe, relationships that governed the behaviour, thinking and life of each individual African."[1]

The plantation system, in which many Africans found themselves, was characterized by gross immorality, inhumanity, and injustice, by moral viciousness and appalling cruelty, especially toward the enslaved. Some of the European slave masters genuinely believed that Africans were an inferior variety of human being, a kind of subhuman species who stood "on a lower evolutionary plane than the white man."[2]

The enslaved people were not permitted to rebuild their lives according to their own familiar African patterns. Moreover, there was very little in their new environment that could even begin to replace what they had lost, little that could inspire or enlighten them concerning the importance of family or, at an even more fundamental level, the intrinsic worth and value of the human being.

So severe and long-lasting was the impact of all this that Richard Hart referred to "the formidable historical legacy of a widespread lack of racial self-respect" on the part of the African-Jamaican people in the 1920s and 30s.[3]

* * *

This is where one would have expected the church to make a difference. Christianity has the potential to profoundly impact believers by its revelation of our value and worth in God's eyes. This revelation provides powerful motivation for moral transformation. Could there be something lacking in our presentation of the gospel, some basic flaw that time and repetition have institutionalized and that has distorted our understanding of the gospel? I believe there is.

The flaw lies in what we fail to emphasize when we preach the gospel; namely, that in the beginning, God created us good. Instead, we tend to give the impression that God's primary message to us is that we are sinners.

As a result, our hearers see sinfulness as their original condition. They accept sin as the attribute that spiritually identifies them. They conclude, then, that God's main disposition to human beings is one of anger and disapproval.

But we did not originate in sin; we originated in the mind of the Creator. God designed us for a close, personal relationship with Himself. Sin was the result of the enemy's efforts to ruin the great design of the Creator. However depraved we may have become, God recognizes our potential; He sees what He originally invested in us. He would never hold a low opinion of those whom He created in His image, for His glory.

Something must be seriously wrong with teaching that affirms a person's low self-image of being good for nothing, teaching that fails to address people's deep-seated self-hatred and sense of hopelessness.

As a Bible study teacher and camp counselor for over 45 years, I have become increasingly aware of this tendency towards self-hatred and hopelessness that dominates many of my fellow-Jamaicans. As part of a personal strategy to counteract this trend, I have used storytelling as a tool for creating awareness of the issue. The stories are meant to make hearers aware of a major misconception that they have about Christianity. The misconception is this: the first thing that God wants us to know is that we are sinners. By contrast, the main story, The Garden Shrub, seeks to highlight the truth of our immense value in God's eyes, a truth that underlies the whole gospel message.

As you read this story, consider how it presents a different way of understanding the gospel.

THE GARDEN SHRUB

Once upon a time there was a master gardener. He didn't just have green fingers; he was a brilliant plant geneticist who had produced several hybrid plants of outstanding quality.

His fame spread abroad and reached the ears of the most powerful and wealthy king on earth. This king was known to have the finest royal gardens in the world.

One day the king sent a message to the master gardener: "As you know, I have in my collection every known kind and variety of plants to be found on the face of the earth. But I have a great desire for a new plant never seen before, a magnificent, breathtaking, beautiful shrub, which will be the marvel and envy of all the gardeners and kings of this world. I believe you have what it takes to create such a plant."

When the master gardener received this message his heart leapt for joy. He was facing the greatest challenge of his life, but it was a grand opportunity. The master gardener determined to pour everything he had into this project—all his skill, experience, and inspiration. He outdid himself; the result was a masterpiece.

Then tragedy struck. The day came for the plant to be delivered to the king. That morning, very early, the master gardener went out to his greenhouse to take one last look at his masterpiece. But the plant was gone. A thief had broken in and stolen it during the night.

It is impossible to describe the feelings of the master gardener. With haste he closed down his greenhouse, said goodbye to family and friends, and went off in search of his masterpiece. The search lasted 10 years. At last he found it. He was only just in time. It turned out that an envious rival horticulturist had stolen the plant, intending to propagate and sell as many as possible. The thief knew the value of this remarkable shrub and hoped to become a millionaire. But his efforts to propagate were a failure. He lacked the knowledge and the skill needed to handle this unique specimen. After years of trying, he finally gave up and threw out the overgrown, bedraggled original plant. It had suffered greatly at the hands of the ignorant mercenary thief. It was a wonder the plant was still alive.

Two days after the frustrated thief had thrown out the dying plant, the master gardener came by. The plant was lying on top of a load of garbage in the city dump when the master gardener saw it. No one would have given it a second look. But, from the moment he set eyes on the miserable wreck, the master gardener recognized his masterpiece. His heart leapt for joy, for he already knew just what he would do to restore the precious shrub to its former glory.

For What Purpose Was I Made?

As a Christian I can identify with the plant, for I too was stolen and abused by the enemy and rescued by the Lord at great personal cost.

But the story does not begin with that tragedy. That is not the first thing we learn about the plant. Instead, the story begins by placing great emphasis on the purpose for which the plant was first designed and created. It is this fact that makes sense of the rest of the story. That very special hybrid plant was made for the king's palace. It could not be allowed to go to waste, rotting away on a garbage dump.

We are like that special plant. God rescued us from the garbage dump because we don't belong there. As our Creator, He understands that better than we do. It is He who made us, not for the junkyard, but for His palace.

When we preach the gospel beginning with the point of our sinfulness, it is possible to give the false impression that the life God gave us included sin as a component of our original design. Consequently, many Christians have a deep fear of failure, even a fear of losing their salvation, no matter what they do. They fear that sooner or later they will revert to their original condition, as they understand it, that is, a state of sinfulness. For them, a sinless life is not possible. Transformation and grace are secondary components of their theology instead of primary.

This is the danger of teaching about sin outside of the context of our God-given identity. The truth is that we began in the mind of God, before the creation of the world, as perfect beings. God designed us for Himself. We were originally made for the palace.

This then is the good news: God has taken the initiative to ensure that we are restored to our true original purpose and perfect condition. Salvation means full restoration.

As we shall see, it makes a world of difference to our self-image and our understanding of the gospel to know who we really are, where we are coming from, and the purpose for which we were made. The story of the Dani people, in the next chapter, is an outstanding example of what happens when our understanding of the gospel is based on the biblical reality of these basic concerns.

---

[1] Hazel Bennett and Philip Sherlock, *The Story of the Jamaican People* (Jamaica: Ian Randle Publishers, 1998), 126.

[2] *Encyclopaedia Britannica*, 11th ed., s.v. "Negro."

[3] Richard Hart, *Slaves Who Abolished Slavery* (Jamaica: University of the West Indies Press, 2002), i.

THREE

TELL ME YOUR ORIGIN STORY

WHERE ARE WE COMING FROM?

THE DANI PEOPLE ARE A TRIBAL GROUP LIVING IN IRIAN JAYA ON THE ISLAND of New Guinea. When missionaries from the Western world first arrived among them in the middle of the 20th century, they found a truly Stone Age people, with only stone tools and no written language.

In his book *Torches of Joy*, John Dekker tells how he and his wife Helen arrived in Irian Jaya from Canada in 1960 and settled among the Danis.[1] As John worked with the men on various projects and learnt more and more of their language, he began asking them questions about their beliefs: "What is your origin? Where did your forefathers come from?"

The men told John that their ancestors, together with all living creatures, had come up out of a hole in the ground, far away in the place where the sun rises. They described how these living creatures had managed to cross "a great water" by walking on the body of a long snake that obligingly arched itself like a bridge over the water. Thus their ancestors arrived at where they now lived.

John listened with interest, then shared stories of the origin of life from the Western world. Finally, he told them what he himself believed, based on the teaching of the Bible, beginning at Genesis 1.

"God created everything," he told them. "God made us like Himself so that we might have fellowship with Him. Our forefathers knew this truth, but they wanted to do things their own way. They were deceived by evil spirits and no longer taught their children about God. After many generations, the knowledge of God was lost.

"Even so, God still loved His people, the ones He had created. He came into this world. He became like one of us. When He grew up, He taught us; He showed us what God was like. Then He proved His love for us by taking the punishment for our wrongdoing upon Himself. He died for us, but He came back to life. He said that He was returning to Heaven but that He would come to earth again. In the meantime, we are to tell everyone about His love and His ways."

John did not expect the Danis to take in all of this teaching straight away. When he saw how eager, curious, and interested they were, he arranged classes four days a week and began taking them through the gospel message step by step.

The Danis were intrigued and deeply impressed with the new idea that God created everything, and especially that He had made human beings in His image. When John pointed out that he and they were related because they all had the same forefathers, it blew their minds. The news spread from village to village. Even after he had been teaching them other truths, they kept coming back to the primary question of their origin: "Tell us again how we are made in God's image and how we have the same ancestors as you," they requested when John joined their firesides in the evenings.

In a remarkable way that basic truth became the main point of reference for every aspect of the teaching. For example, John taught them that God loved them and He had not forgotten them, though they had forgotten Him. John taught that his presence among them was evidence of this: "He prepared me to come and tell you about God the Creator. God spoke to me and said, 'Others are made in My image; you must go and tell them about Me.'"

John also described to them the character of God as we see it in Jesus—holy and good and kind. Then he said: "Remember last week I taught you that all of us are made in the image of God. God made you to be like Him. You are important to God. He wants you to be His child and to be just like Him. Our forefather Adam was kind and good at first, but he lost this goodness because he sinned in the garden. Traces of the Creator's likeness are still in you, even though your people have long forgotten about God."

When John wanted to motivate them to live in unity with each other, he reminded them of the same basic truth: "We are not to steal from each other. We are not to kill each other. We are to respect each other because we are all made in the image of God. God loves people, and we should love them, too."

On another occasion, John related the story of the Good Samaritan, adding, "The Creator taught that we should help other people, not just those in our own clan. We are to care for one another. We are to be a blessing to others. Because we are made in His image, we are to do as He would do."

Wuninip, a young, strong, able warrior and leader among the Danis, became one of John's keenest and most articulate pupils. In the newly built circular teaching house, Wuninip was among the first of John's students. They were all men, ranging in age from teens to mid-forties and squatting on leaves or pieces of wood on the ground. Their skin was smudged black and greasy; markings were scratched on their faces and upper torsos, and glistening boar tusks pierced their noses. Their long hair was held in nets, and they were naked, apart from ornamental armbands and pubic gourds.

As the weeks of teaching continued, Wuninip attended faithfully. When John asked a question in class and Wuninip answered, the answer was always well thought out, spoken rapidly and persuasively. When Wuninip spoke, people were quiet and listened.

John and his wife, Helen, began to see a difference in the way the Dani walked and talked. But several months passed before Wuninip knew he was a new creature in Christ. John realized it when he heard Wuninip pray, "O Creator, greetings! I come to You in appreciation that You have made me in Your image. I thank You that You brought John to us. I thank You for forgiving my sins."

Even as Wuninip acknowledged and welcomed God's gift of forgiveness, his prayer bore witness to the fact that humanity's creation in God's image is basic to the divine plan of salvation.

As events later showed, the knowledge of the truth brought about radical change in the lives of Wuninip and others like him. John was an innovative teacher. He planted a patch of weeds and said to his students: "These weeds represent sins you used to commit. This weed is stealing. We'll cut it off, because you don't steal anymore. This one is lying. We'll cut it off, since you don't lie anymore. This one is war; this one is murder; this one is rape. Now they are all cut off, all gone. Will these plants come up again?"

"Of course they will."

"But they're gone. Why do you say they will come up again?"

"Because the roots are still there."

"Do these sins still have roots in your hearts? Could these sins come into your lives again?" John asked.

"Yes, they could," the Danis affirmed.

"What is the main root of sin in your hearts?" John asked. They couldn't answer right away. "Think about it and talk it over while I go to the medical hut for half an hour."

When John returned, one man spoke for the group. "We know that our main root of sin is our pride. We Dani men are very proud. We do all sorts of things to show off for the women. At feasts, we wear our long ceremonial gourds and swing our hair back and forth to impress the women. We spend much time greasing our long hair to draw attention to ourselves." The men talked abut pride for some time. Then they prayed together, confessing their sin to the Lord.

Later that same day, Wuninip and Kininip, another leader, came to John. "Will you please cut our long hair?"

"I can't do that. Why do you want to cut your hair?"

"Tolibaga, remember this morning we identified our pride as our worst root of sin. We feel that our long hair is a symbol of our pride. With it we attract attention to ourselves rather than to God. We must cut our long hair."

"Wait a minute; this is drastic thing to do in your culture. You'd better pray about it."

"Tolibaga, we have prayed, and we know we must do this."

"Then you must do it yourselves."

"We have no scissors. May we borrow yours?"

Taking the scissors, the men disappeared into the chicken yard, behind the seven-foot fence. Forty-five minutes later they reappeared, looking very self-conscious. Helen was startled. "What happened to Wuninip and Kininip?" John quickly explained. "Wait until the village people see them!"

Wuninip and Kininip set out for the village. Along the way, startled Danis asked the same question. "What happened to your hair?" Wide-eyed children scurried ahead to the village to tell their elders.

"What will our friends say?" Kininip and Wuninip wondered as they walked. Anxiety coursed through Kininip. "Wuninip can return to his house near Tolibaga, but I have to live in the village," he thought. But Kininip didn't regret his action. Each man prayed for courage to explain why he had cut his hair. Both men prayed that the God who had showed them their pride would speak to others, too.

When the men arrived at the village, the people were watching for them. They crowded around to hear what the two had to say.

"Tolibaga gave us a lesson about the roots of sin in our hearts. He asked us, 'What is the main root of your sin?' We didn't answer right away. He left us for a while, and we talked it over. Then we decided that pride is our main sin. Our long hair is what we are most proud of, so we cut it off. God has made us in His likeness that we might show forth His character—not draw attention to ourselves."

Some shook their heads in dismay. Others faintly understood. Some began to examine their own hearts.

In huts throughout the Kanggime area, Danis talked about the believers who had cut their long hair. Some were convicted about their lives and motives. Slowly a change came over the Toli Valley. Whereas before only a few had followed the Lord, now many were turning to God, realizing what He had done for them by sending His Son.

"It is as if we are living in a different world," John wrote to the mission staff and supporters. "The atmosphere has completely changed. People have started to love one another. They have confessed their wrongs of the past—stealing, killing pigs, killing persons. They now want to make it right, not only by asking forgiveness but also by making restitution where possible."

What a remarkable story! The miraculous change in the Dani people all began with a teaching based on a right understanding of our identity in God. The story of the Dani people illustrates how essential it is to begin at the beginning when sharing the gospel. Let's now consider what it means to begin at the beginning.

---

1 John Dekker and Lois Neely, *Torches of Joy* (Seattle, WA: Ywam Publishing, 1996), Used with permission.

FOUR

BEGIN AT THE BEGINNING

WHERE IS THE BEGINNING? IT IS FOUND IN THE FIRST CHAPTERS OF GENESIS. There we find the answers to the primary questions of life, such as: Who am I? What are my spiritual roots? For what purpose was I created?

The opening chapters of Genesis also lay the foundation for the gospel. The first two chapters describe our spiritual origins. They define our spiritual identity and purpose. In so doing, they reveal how valuable we are in God's eyes. Chapter 3 follows with the story of humanity's disobedience, which led to separation from God and from the good life in the Garden of Eden. The Old Testament Scriptures record the appalling consequences of this disobedience for future generations. At the same time, these Scriptures reveal God's desire and purpose to forgive and transform sinful humans and to restore our broken relationship with Him.

Yet nothing quite prepares us for the way in which He eventually carried out this purpose. In the New Testament we learn of Jesus' astounding act of self-sacrifice for our sake. By giving His life, the Son of God Himself rescued us from our predicament. His action on behalf of the disobedient and the depraved is credible only because of what we learn in Genesis 1 and 2. We are valuable in God's eyes. Therefore Genesis 1 and 2 provide the rationale for His amazing grace.

We speak of the human predicament in terms of a fall. Humanity fell. There never was a fall as tragic, a fall with consequences as serious as humanity's fall in the Garden of Eden. The seriousness of a fall depends on the height from which the fall takes place. Humanity fell from the highest place accorded any created being; that is, a flawless image of God and perfect fellowship with Him.

If we are to take sin seriously and know and feel the tragedy of the fall of humanity, we must become fully aware of our original creation in the image of God and all that it means. These are truths the enemy may want us to be ignorant of, gloss over, or take for granted. The reason is plain. Conviction of sin results more effectively from sin preached in the context of Genesis 1 and 2 than from preaching that begins at Genesis 3, the story of humanity's fall. I learnt this myself from personal experience.

My Beginning

More than 35 years ago, in 1970, I "discovered" Genesis 1 and 2. I had been asked to conduct a series of Bible studies under the theme "Male and female in the Bible," and these two chapters provided material of fundamental significance to the theme.

All of us who engaged in these studies had an unforgettable experience. Among other things, we found it mind-blowing to learn that our sexuality was rooted in the divine image, for we were created male and female in the image of God (Genesis 1:26, 27).

In the years following that experience, I had several opportunities to share the wonderful insights embedded in these chapters.

On one occasion, I was invited to speak on Genesis 1 and 2 at a series of meetings arranged by a fairly large church in Kingston, Jamaica. On the third evening, a Tuesday, I dealt with the story in Genesis 2 that tells how woman came into being. I paid special attention to the process (verses 19-23) by which the man was prepared in advance to recognize, welcome, and appreciate the woman when she appeared—a process that highlights the fact of our having been made for relationship.

The following morning, the pastor of the church where I was speaking had a visit from a young man. He told the pastor that he had heard the presentation on Genesis 2 the evening before. That night he could not sleep. The story of the way Eve had come into Adam's life and the way Adam welcomed and appreciated her had made a profound impression on him. He was deeply disturbed and strongly convicted of his own attitude and treatment of women. The man declared, "I cannot continue living the way I am living now."

Later, the pastor remarked on how ready and eager the young man had been to turn his life over to the Lord Jesus.

The story of this young man gives me hope. His conversion opened my eyes to the evangelistic potential of Genesis 1 and 2. It illustrates the potential of Genesis 2 to specifically address the breakdown in the relationship between men and women in our society. What astounded me was the fact that during my presentation of Genesis 2, I had made no mention of sin or sinful practices. I was not even trying to be "evangelistic," yet that young man was strongly convicted of sin.

His experience made sense. I had presented to him God's ideal, dream, and vision for us, His children, and for our relationships. That vision made the young man extremely uncomfortable, as though he were wearing shabby clothing and seated next to someone immaculately dressed. He saw that he did not measure up to God's ideal in his relationships.

The contrast between God's design for humankind and the present human condition created acute discomfort and deep longing in him. In this contrast lies the power of true conviction of sin.

EVANGELISM THE ROMAN WAY

As we have already seen, the experience of the Danis shows how important it is to begin at Genesis 1 and 2 when teaching the gospel to those who have no previous knowledge of the Bible. On the other hand, the story of the young Jamaican man shows how relevant these chapters can be to those already familiar with the gospel. In Jamaica, like this young man many have grown up with some Christian teaching, but their lives show little or no evidence of it. Genesis 1 and 2 may be just what is needed to stir a response from them. These two chapters lay a foundation, provide a context, and bring a perspective that is indispensable for understanding the gospel.

However, there are those who point out that they are following biblical precedent when they preach the gospel beginning at Genesis 3. Though the Bible itself begins with Genesis 1 and 2, they omit the teaching found in these chapters and start instead with humanity's sinful condition. They do so because some of the most outstanding sermons recorded in Scripture begin in this way.

Without a doubt, since the fall of humankind, repentance forms the main thrust of the message sent by God to His people, as recorded in the Scriptures. The Old Testament is full of such messages. The biblical preaching of repentance is a call to turn away from sin, with detailed reference to the kinds of sinful practices that God hates.

Then in the New Testament, when John the Baptist is preparing the way for Jesus' coming, he thunders against sin and calls on his hearers, high and low, rich and poor, to repent. Jesus Himself begins His ministry with a call to repentance.

It is in the moving and magnificent letter of Paul to the Romans that we find the sinfulness of human nature under God's wrath described more elaborately and forcefully than anywhere else in the New Testament. Well might we be awestruck at the power of Paul's writing and moved to imitate his approach! Perhaps, therefore, it is not surprising that many Christians today have adopted as their preferred approach to evangelism a model that they call the Roman Way, based on Romans 1-3. A main feature of this evangelistic approach is the effort to convince the hearer that he is a sinner under the wrath of God, as the first step in the evangelistic process.

Without a doubt, there are cases where it is appropriate to begin by confronting persons with the fact of their lawlessness and rebellion against God. However, it is clear from the life of Jesus, the experience of Paul and missionaries such as John Dekker, that such an evangelistic approach is not the only suitable one in every case. Moreover, to call this approach the Roman Way raises significant questions for me.

How justified are we in using this letter of Paul as a model for evangelizing the untaught and the unbelieving? Was that Paul's purpose in writing this letter? Was the letter addressed to the untaught and unbelieving? Clearly it was not.

THE ROMAN READERS AND PAUL'S PURPOSE

Paul's letter was written to Christians, "to all in Rome who are loved by God and called to be saints" (1:7). These were persons who had already heard and responded to the gospel. They were not unbelievers; they were fellow-Christians, well groomed in the faith. Many were Jews who had accepted Jesus as the Messiah. The majority were evidently Gentiles, many of whom would quite possibly have come to accept Christianity by way of previous conversion to Judaism. They would all have been well taught in the Hebrew Scriptures. We are not justified in using Paul's letter to the Romans as a model for reaching unbelievers. Paul was not preaching to the unconverted; he was not "evangelizing."

If Paul did not write his letter to the Romans to bring unbelievers to the faith, then what was his purpose? Why did he devote so much space and energy to convincing his readers of their sinful condition?

Paul knew his readers well. He was one of them. Raised as a Jew, well schooled in the teachings and traditions of Judaism, he was keenly observant of the Law. He also knew the besetting sin that he shared with many like himself—the sin of self-righteousness and spiritual pride. For Paul, the tremendous change that his conversion brought about was the reversal of this pride and a transformed understanding of human righteousness. In letting go of his pride, Paul came to count as rubbish the attributes he had valued so highly before (Philippians 3:3-8).

Abandoning these props and becoming convinced of the depth of his sinfulness (1 Timothy 1:15), Paul turned to clothe himself with the righteousness Christ provided for him. He now understood that he had no power to acquire or deserve this righteousness.

This was the change of heart Paul wanted for his hearers. As someone who identified with them, he knew that this was the change they needed most of all. Paul's task in the letter to the Romans was to remind his Jewish audience that they were sinners like everyone else. It would not be an easy task, for the Jews prided themselves on being separate, privileged, and distinct from unbelieving Gentiles and pagans. He also felt impelled to impress on them that God's righteousness offered in Christ was a free gift, to be received by faith. In the past, they had been trying to establish their own righteousness by their own effort, by observing the demands of the Law.

It was a monumental task, a seemingly impossible reversal, hence the energy, wealth of illustration, and complexity of argument that Paul brings to the task.

PAUL'S LETTER: A CHALLENGE, AN INSPIRATION

Reading Romans today, we might well be captivated by Paul's passion and compelling rhetoric. No wonder we want to emulate him, to

Faith Linton

copy his model, to bring conviction to our audience by the same method. Yet in our zeal and excitement to imitate Paul, we must be careful not to overlook the circumstances of the lives of Paul and his readers and the conditions on which his approach was based.

It was out of Paul's knowledge of his readers and shared experiences that he could write with much insight and such depth of feeling. From this shared knowledge and teaching he drew his cogent arguments, expecting and knowing that his readers would understand his line of reasoning.

What of ourselves? When we minister to others, do we take time to know them first? Are we acquainted with their belief systems, their world view? Is there anything that we have in common with them, any level at which we identify with them? Are we prepared to engage with them at the point of their deepest need?

REVISITING THE DANI

The story of John Dekker and the Danis illustrates what can happen when a missionary seeks to know those to whom he is ministering. John and his wife, Helen, settled among the Dani. They did not visit for a brief "evangelistic" crusade and then leave. They settled among them. John worked with the men on various projects and learned their language, laying the groundwork of trust and understanding, earning the right to ask them questions about their beliefs. John listened to their origin stories. He then shared stories of the origin of life from the Western world. It was a mutual sharing, a balanced exchange, of respect for each other. Only then did John tell the Dani what he himself believed, beginning at the Creation story of Genesis 1. He continued with the story of human sin and God's sacrifice to restore us, and ended with Christ's commission to invite everyone to believe.

Having secured their interest, John arranged regular classes with the Dani. He found that they kept returning to the same story. This became the lever, the basic truth that John used to bring home to the Dani just what their relationships and behaviour should be like: "God made you to be like Him; this is what God is like, and therefore you also must be loving, truthful, and honest."

How different this approach is from that of the currently practised Roman Way. And how effective it was! If the story of the Dani demon-

42

strates anything, it is that in presenting the gospel, it is wise to start with the good news that God created us in His image. That is where the Scriptures begin. That is where the hearers of the Old Testament prophets would have begun their faith journey, and so would the Roman readers of Paul's letter.

The good news of the truths revealed in the first two chapters of Scripture form the basis on which the Jews' spiritual heritage is built.

ROMANS 1-3: STRONG MEDICINE

Paul knew from personal experience that God's chosen people had become so strong and confident in their spiritual heritage that they tended to lose sight of their sinfulness and the threat of God's wrath. Instead of measuring themselves against God's standard of holiness, they were comparing themselves with others. They took pride in being better than those who were sinners like themselves, declaring, "God, I thank you that I am not like other men" (Luke 18:11). They needed the strong medicine of Romans 1-3 to restore them to a humble dependence on God. They were secure and strong enough in spirit to receive it.

Consider by contrast people we might be seeking to reach today, people living in poverty, ignorance and deprivation, as many are in Jamaica now. What is their greatest need? What is the medicine they require? Is it to be battered by reminders of God's wrath and their own sinfulness? No. Surely they need to hear God's gracious word: "You are mine. I made you in My image. Be transformed in Jesus' name, and do what is right!"

Let there be no misunderstanding. Preaching for conviction of sin will always be necessary, for we are fallen beings, prone to blindness about our sin, saint and sinner alike. What I want to emphasize is that this call to repentance is best done when the foundation is first laid— that our origin is from God, we are God's creation, and our destiny is to be like Him.

God's plan is for us to be like Him. It is His plan, and He is quite determined and dedicated to its success.

REACHING UNBELIEVERS

If not in the letter to the Romans, where might we look for a model to bring unbelievers to faith? In Acts 17 we find Paul beginning to reach out to the Athenians. First, he observed their way of life—sophisticated philosophy, love of discussion, and many idols. Their idolatry moved and distressed him. He engaged with them in their discussions and won their respect, so they invited him to speak at their center of learning. When he spoke, he began on common ground and referred to what he had learned of them. He spoke out of his understanding and respect for them. He took the opening provided by their altar inscribed "to an unknown god," and in this way he did not antagonize them by directly targeting their many idols (Acts 17:23). Paul began with wisdom and discretion, and no doubt his hearers warmed to him because they sensed his caring, deep distress at their spiritual condition. Paul's talk focused on the nature of God as Creator and God's purpose for humanity. When he spoke of repentance, it was in reference to their ignorance of God's nature—what Paul believed was their area of greatest need.

This is the same evangelistic approach as the Dekkers used with the Danis. They began with a time of observing and learning about the people, followed by times of engaging with them in their chosen activities. In this way they earned respect and the right to share stories and beliefs. Then they shared the gospel, beginning with the good news of Genesis 1.

OUTREACH IN JAMAICA AND THE CARIBBEAN

I believe that many of those to whom we now preach the gospel lack just what the ancient Athenians lacked—a heightened awareness of the one true God and of themselves as He originally designed them. They lack a sense of kinship, of belonging to their Creator, and therefore of what they owe to Him. They do not know the significance of their creation in His image. Consequently they have no clear, healthy sense of their spiritual identity (such as the Jews had) or of the purpose for which they were created. If the message we preach to them does not attempt to fill this gap, their understanding of the gospel will be distorted. They may be driven to repentance out of fear of Hell. They may seek self-centered satisfaction and happiness by allying themselves with Christ. But they will not be motivated to please God. Why? Because the gospel message they have received does not allow them to see how closely connected they are to God, who made them in His image. So they will continue to feel alienated from Him. They will feel unable to relate closely to Him. My own personal experience bears this out.

FIVE

A DAMAGED MASTERPIECE

BY THE TIME I WAS 16 YEARS OLD, MY PERSONAL ORIGIN STORY WAS WELL established in my own mind, and I wasn't comfortable with it. I am a brown-skinned Jamaican. The color of my skin together with my knowledge of my country's history told me two things about myself: some of my ancestors were enslaved Africans; some were Caucasian.

In the 1930s and 1940s, when my brother, my twin sister and I grew up, Jamaican society was divided into separate and distinct worlds. First in order of importance, though numerically the minority, were the whites. They owned most of the arable land and dominated the legislature and the professions. Their children were fluent in Standard English, attended the best schools, either in Jamaica or England, and enjoyed a lifestyle similar to that of the British upper-middle class. In other words, they were highly favored, and we yearned to be in their shoes.

Last in order of importance, though numerically in the majority, were the blacks. They mostly eked a precarious living out of the soil and were available for all the menial or low-paying jobs. Their children attended the local elementary school (of which the favored whites never darkened the doors), were fluent only in patois, enjoyed the pleasures of Anancy stories and mento music, indulged in pocomania, sought the illicit services of the obeah man, and suffered the disadvantages of a permanently damaged family structure.

Between these two ends of the social continuum there was a wide range of tradesmen and skilled workers, small but successful farmers, shopkeepers, struggling entrepreneurs, poorly paid clerks, office workers, and professionals, such as teachers and nurses. All shades of color were represented in this group. They were the socially mobile, enterprising, hard-working backbone of the society, but they were not a homogeneous group. An intricate and complex set of distinctions separated them. For example, prestige could depend on being light-skinned with straight or wavy hair, rather than on academic qualification or money.

MARRIAGE, COLOR, AND CLASS

One highly-prized mark of social distinction was legally married parents. My sister and I prided ourselves on the fact that as far back as we were aware, for three generations at least, marriage had been the norm on both sides of the family. At the same time, we knew that somewhere further back in the past there must have been an unholy union between black and white. In our minds, there were no romantic overtones to relieve the evidence of the history books that in the days of slavery such unions were often brutal, degraded affairs.

The idea that I resulted from such an affair, though it would have happened generations earlier, caused me shame and discomfort, mainly because of the continuing stigma attached to slavery and its concomitants.

I could see no farther than the degradation. At that time, in the 1930s and 1940s, Marcus Garvey's ideas had not yet received general acclaim and acceptance. We learnt little in school about the achievements of blacks, and Africa was still considered the Dark Continent in every sense of the term. Indeed we were encouraged to look to England as the mother country. For me, England represented a condescending, disdainful foster mother.

Two experiences conspired to establish my status as a second-class half-caste, one in the family setting, the other in high school. My parents, both trained teachers from similar backgrounds, differed in one important aspect. One was dark-skinned, the other very light-skinned. Some of my father's fair-skinned family regretted the marriage simply on the basis of color, while members of my mother's family rejoiced that her children would be lighter in complexion than she was. I distinctly remember attending a family wedding and being cold-shouldered by my father's cousins. Where did I really belong? As the saying goes, I was neither fish, flesh, fowl nor good red herring. I faced a crisis of identity. My high school experience provided unwelcome answers.

At age 12, my twin sister and I won scholarships to St. Hilda's, a girls' boarding school in the hills beyond the island's north coast. The school was a transplant direct from Britain. The headmistress was a native of Chichester, England, and an Oxford graduate. Most of the pupils at that time were the white or fair-skinned children of Jamaica's social elite. At St. Hilda's my identity was clearly defined. I was placed in a dormitory reserved for children of doubtful social origin, children who had attended the elementary school, probably had difficulty with the English language, and were deficient in the social graces. I now knew just where I stood. I could see how short I fell of the social ideal; I knew the full measure of the unworthiness of my origins.

A JOYLESS RELIGION

What role did my Christian faith have in all this? Beginning in the womb, God-consciousness had always been a major feature of my life. I grew up with godly parents. As soon as my father heard the news of our birth, he fell on his knees and dedicated his twin daughters to God. My mother's relationship with God was close, warm, and personal. In the small rural community where we lived the influence of the church was dominant.

Even before we entered our teens, my sister and I had developed the habit of daily prayer and Bible reading. But ours was a joyless, dutiful religion. Our main impression of God was that of an awesome, far-off, all-knowing Being who never overlooked the smallest misdeed. Even while we despaired of ever attaining His standards of perfection, we felt duty bound to strive toward doing so.

It was a religion that offered no dissent and no relief from the sense of alienation and unworthiness instilled by the class- and color-conscious society in which we were being raised.

So far we had missed the main message of Christianity, a message that my mother already knew from experience—above everything else, God desires relationship with us.

When that truth first dawned on my consciousness, the eagerness of my response was muted by the deeply ingrained conviction of alienation and unworthiness. This unworthiness derived not only from my sinful condition. I knew that at the spiritual level I was alienated from God because of sin. I also knew that Christ, in great mercy, had dealt with the sin problem; I received His full and final provision with deep gratitude. But there still remained a fundamental source of alienation and unworthiness—my social origins. Nothing could change that. I was forever unworthy, forever alienated both from a highly favored social and racial elite and, moreover, from an infinitely high and holy God. I was an outsider. I just did not belong. Relationship, approval, and acceptance still eluded me.

But God had started a process, one that He would complete. It was a thoroughgoing re-education process—what the Bible calls a renewing of the mind (Romans 12:2).

SIX

PROCESS OF RESTORATION

AFTER MY DISCOVERY OF THE MESSAGE OF GENESIS 1:26 AND 27 IN THE summer of 1970, it was as if a whole world of implications and applications began to open up for me. As I meditated on the manifestation of the divine image reflected in humankind, I was struck by the endless variety and diversity of this manifestation. Not only did humans come in a variety of colors, shapes and sizes, personalities, and temperaments, each person within each national group was also different from the other. We could point to every individual and say, "There has never been, there is not, and there will never be another person exactly like you." Each one was unique. What did this mean?

The conclusion seemed obvious. The infinite God, who has no beginning and no end, can never come to an end of expressing who He is. Each human being provides an opportunity for God to express Himself in a new way, through yet another unique manifestation of His image.

Applying this personally, several things became clear. I am not just the product of circumstances, cruel or obscure. My presence in the world is a statement of eternal significance, a statement never quite expressed in this way before. The circumstances of my ancestry and racial-social history might be flawed, but that is the nature of things in a fallen world.

I myself am flawed, but now I know that my sinful condition does not define me.

I have a spiritual identity, a spiritual history; and my spiritual history is not rooted in sin. I originated in the mind of God, even before the creation of the world.

He designed me with a particular purpose in mind: to be the pinnacle of His creation, to be among His representatives, His stewards in charge of all the earth. That design and purpose came first. Nothing that sin, Satan, or society has done, or can do, will ultimately defeat the original plan and purpose of God. Indeed, the process of restoration has already begun—the restoration of my ruined condition to its original beauty and perfection.

The true story of my origins and the continuing spiritual history in Christ is more wonderfully affirming than I could ever ask or think.

It has been more than 35 years since these truths first burst upon my consciousness, and they continue to blow my mind and bring tears to my eyes. The repercussions of this breakthrough have been far-reaching. The alienation, the sense that I did not really belong, the feeling of unworthiness, had produced resentment and mistrust in me toward God. This, in turn, blocked and hindered growth in my relationship with Him and in Christian character.

Yet, at the same time, I was growing in knowledge and understanding of the Scriptures and rejoiced in what I was learning. I enjoyed nothing more than sharing the great truths of the Bible. There was never any question in my mind about the miracle of the new birth that had taken place in my life. I was aware of the Holy Spirit's work in me. But I kept coming up against a barrier that blocked the release into the freedom and joy of knowing that I was loved unconditionally, accepted totally, approved of, delighted in—because I belonged.

My experience over the past 35 years has been one of continuing and increasing release. Each time I have shared the message of Genesis 1 and 2 with others, the assurance of my value and worth in God's eyes has strengthened and deepened. Little by little, I have been receiving a completely new perception of myself, my identity, and my significance, coming from the hand of the Creator who invested Himself in me when He made me in His image.

Who am I? Where do I belong? I am no longer in doubt, confusion, and shame because of the answers to these questions. So-called disadvantages of race, color, and social class have increasingly lost their importance, their power to crush my spirit.

At the same time, I have been amazed and horrified at the strength and persistence of the deep-seated sense of alienation and unworthiness within me. Radical change takes time. The journey into wholeness has been ongoing for the last 50 years. For the most part it has been exhilarating, but not always so.

Let me share with you some of the highlights of this ongoing work of change, healing and deliverance that is being accomplished in me by the Spirit of God, largely as a result of the message of Genesis 1 and 2.

A PAINFUL DELIVERANCE

In about 1978, eight years after the initial breakthrough when I first "discovered" the message of Genesis 1 and 2, I attended a meeting featuring Jimmy Smith, a visiting North American Christian speaker. He came at a time when the Charismatic renewal was at its height in Jamaica. He himself had a special gift, a special ministry. A talented pianist and singer, he used his gifts to lead others into a rich experience of worship. It was at that meeting that my eyes were opened to the block in my spirit preventing me from releasing myself into worship.

I asked for an appointment to speak with him. The night before the appointment, I found myself going back over my life. The memories of past experiences were vivid and strong. The following afternoon I met with Jimmy Smith, together with his host and hostess in Jamaica, Bert and Frances Armstrong, an Irish Methodist minister and his wife whom I knew and loved. They were all people of prayer.

Jimmy began by questioning me about my life history. The vivid memories of the previous evening provided the answers. He took notes as I spoke. Then, when he felt he had heard enough, he began to deal, one by one, with what he perceived to be the causes of the problem. There were five. Three causes were teachers, all women, who had exercised undue and harmful influence over me, one when I was a schoolgirl, one when I was a student in France, and one when I was actually a teacher myself. The two other causes were negative and harmful perceptions I had internalized about myself.

Each time Jimmy named one of these five causes, an extraordinary thing happened. A strange sound spiraled from my throat, continued out and beyond my body, then faded out of sight. I was somehow aware that my own vocal chords were not involved in making the sound. Each time the sound faded, Jimmy led in prayer, dealing with issues such as repentance, renouncement of evil, affirmation of the good, healing, renewal, and offering forgiveness. It was particularly hard to deal with the feelings associated with my experiences of social ostracism and prejudice.

Why had it been such a challenge to deal with the issue of social ostracism and prejudice? Was it that the grip of evil in this case had been particularly strong? Had I so totally embraced society's distorted perception of my identity that it had become part of me, like a parasitic growth?

At the end of the session, I felt dazed and bewildered. Something spiritually and emotionally significant had happened to me—that I knew. What I did not know was that the battle had just begun. For the next few days I experienced what I can only describe as a taste of Hell. Pandora's box had been opened. A hornet's nest of dark spirits had been disturbed. I fought the forces of evil, rebuking them in Jesus' name.

More difficult to deal with than the demonic hosts were my feelings. I can hardly describe them. A nameless horror filled my mind, and I could not find my way out. I told no one what I was going through.

On the Sunday following the deliverance session, I accompanied my husband to a small mission church in the hills of St. Ann. There were verses of Scripture painted on the walls of the building, and this one caught my eye: "Do not fear, for I am with you; do not be dismayed, for I am your God. I will strengthen you and help you" (Isaiah 41:10).

Light gleamed in the darkness. I knew God had spoken directly to me in my extreme need. After a few days, life gradually returned to normal once again.

For weeks afterwards, I mulled over these events in my mind. How had evil managed to become so entrenched within me? I had lived such a sheltered life, carefully shielded and protected by my parents from moral degradation, the occult, gossip, and loose talk. If this could have happened to me, what of those who were exposed to gross evil? I felt a strong compassion and desire to offer to others the kind of ministry I had received.

SEVEN

FIT TO BE LOVED

became more and more evident that the message of Genesis 1 and 2 was a powerful source of deliverance and healing, especially for those who had a poor sense of self, who doubted their value and worth, in particular as a result of their color, race, or class, even while they maintained their stand as Christians.

I began to see that my value and worth in God's eyes was not reserved just for my soul. I am a complete whole, a unit comprising body, mind, and spirit. Every part of me contributes harmoniously to the unique composition that the Artist-Creator designed me to be. Every part of me was designed to significantly contribute to the special portrait of God's glory seen in me.

Am I short and stocky, brown-skinned, reserved, and inward-looking? Yes, and these are the features, the identifying marks, of this particular masterpiece coming from the hand of the Master Craftsman. If I bemoan the color of my skin, shape of my nose, or kinkiness of my hair, I insult and reject the work of the Creator; I fail to recognize the beauty of His original design and artistry.

In the mid 1980s, I became involved in the work of Youth With A Mission (YWAM), first in Jamaica, where I was invited to speak at their Discipleship Training School year after year. At various times, I have also taught at YWAM bases in Grenada, Guyana, Belize, Barbados, and St. Croix. It was on these occasions that I had the best opportunity and the greatest spiritual freedom to share the message of the first two chapters of the Bible.

In 1990, after a significant time of teaching at the base in Grenada, a time when, as always, the truths I was teaching ministered afresh to me, I prepared to leave for home. In order to be closer to the airport, I stayed overnight in St. George's, at the home of Christian friends, Dhan and Dolly Lalsee. That night I had a dream.

I dreamt that God spoke to me. He said: "Amanda, I will never let you down." It was an experience of awe and wonder, but even in my dream I was puzzled. Why did He call me Amanda? That is not my name! Yet, there was absolutely no doubt in my mind that He was addressing me.

When I woke up, the dream took on even greater reality. I was awe-struck, moved as I had never been before. I continued to be very puzzled about His calling me Amanda. I shared the dream with Dolly, my hostess. Then I asked her if she owned a book of name meanings. She did and went downstairs to look up the name Amanda.

Dolly is normally outgoing and expressive, but on her return upstairs she was curiously silent. She simply held out to me a strip of paper on which was written "Amanda means fit to be loved."

More than 12 years later I am still coming to grips with that statement, still drawing emotional and spiritual nourishment from these words.

I tend to be skeptical. Normally I would have questioned what Dolly had written on that slip of paper. I would have wanted to ascertain for myself that the meaning given was accurate. This time I did not need to do so.

Many years before, when we were teenagers at high school, my twin sister and I had spent an unusual number of hours studying Latin. The Latin teacher, a strangely influential woman, insisted on small classes and extra time for her students. There is no other subject that I remember in as much detail as Latin.

The words "fit to be loved" triggered memories of the conjugation of Latin verbs. *Amandus, amanda, amandum* are the three gender forms (masculine, feminine, neuter) of the gerund, which is the adjective derived, in this case, from the verb *amare*, to love. Whatever the verb, the gerund always means "fit to be." For example, the gerund of the verb *to praise* means "fit to be praised."

Astonishing that, well beforehand, God had put in place with such precision and detail just what was needed to enable me to grasp the full impact of His message.

But more than knowledge of Latin was needed for me to accept the fact that God was actually saying this to me personally, individually. Since 1970, God had been preparing me for this moment by gradually eroding the resistance within me through the consistent application of the message of Genesis 1 and 2 that I am valuable to God. My worth and significance are far greater than I can comprehend; for when He made me in His image, He linked my worth and value to His infinite worth and value. I am loveable, fit to be loved, because of the nature of the God in whose image I am made: His name is Love.

The full significance of all this did not come home to me all at once. The sense of alienation and unworthiness was so deeply entrenched in me that the process of change had, of necessity, to be slow and gradual. Further breakthroughs followed. One in particular stands out in my memory.

In about 1990, a young couple visited our home, bringing their little daughter Sophie, age 7 or 8 years, with them. They were both gifted and well educated. However, their child was very seriously disabled; she could neither walk, talk, nor feed herself. In addition, she was blind. Fortunately, she was able to hear. She was not born like that. She suffered brain damage while undergoing emergency surgery when she was a few weeks old.

We talked about what it meant to take care of Sophie, who needed constant supervision and attention by trained caregivers. As I listened to their story, I was very struck by the attitude of these parents. Their whole life was dominated by the special needs of their child, yet they had chosen to keep her with them, rather than place her in a suitable institution. Instead of being overwhelmed by this difficult situation, they had risen to the challenge in an amazing way. This sadly flawed child seemed to be drawing out of them resources of love, stamina, and creativity that might have remained untapped in a less demanding situation.

For example, Sophie's mother was gifted musically and had a lovely singing voice. Determined to develop the child's limited potential, she composed songs especially for her, which she recorded on audiocassette so that the child could hear them even when her mother was absent.

By this time, as a result of their warmth, acceptance, and devotion, Sophie had grown to know and love her parents. She responded to them with obvious pleasure and trust. She knew them by the sound of their voices, the touch of their hands, and the nearness of their bodies. She also knew when it was a stranger who held her or tried to take care of her, and she would react by becoming quite agitated and unhappy. But she calmed down immediately when Mother or Father came by. They were her lifeline, her source of health and security. To them, she was a special gift, stirring in them a response they did not know they were capable of.

I was deeply impressed. My reaction was: What an object lesson in the value of the human being! Clearly, love is intrinsically bound up with value. We love what we value; we value what we love. Apart from value, love is without substance.

One morning years later, I was reading from the Bible and came upon these words: "The LORD your God is with you, he is mighty to save, he will take great delight in you, he will quiet you with his love, he will rejoice over you with singing" (Zephaniah 3:17).

I recognized these words as a message for me personally, but straightaway I felt the old barriers inside me rise up—barriers of skepticism and disbelief. I wanted, I needed, the kind of affirmation that the passage offered, but I could not find it in myself to receive what God was saying. It did not seem logical to me. How could God take great delight in me? What could He find in me to rejoice over, to sing about? After all, the Bible made it very clear in passages such as Romans 1:18-32 how undesirable and unwholesome we all are because of sin. Indeed, the more I had matured as a Christian, the more aware I had become of how deeply flawed I was.

Over and over in the following weeks and months, I kept coming back to Zephaniah 3:17, this unambiguous statement of how God perceived me. And my reaction would be the same. I could not move beyond the question "What does God see in me?"

Then one day the answer came: "I love you the way Sophie's parents love her."

I wept. I still weep at the unbelievably specific way my question was answered. Every line, every sentence of that verse of Scripture from Zephaniah, had its counterpart in Sophie's life. Her life story "imaged" the truth about God and me.

"The LORD your God is with you." Both Sophie and I were flawed—a distortion of the original "product." A flawed product is usually set aside. Instead, our imperfect condition evoked unexpected commitment and devotion.

"He is mighty to save." Sophie's parents loomed large in her life. Thanks to them, she did not deteriorate into total unresponsiveness. She was rescued from mental and emotional atrophy by their creative attentiveness.

"He will take great delight in you." Given the severe nature of Sophie's disability, every little sign of progress became a major triumph, a source of delight for her parents.

"He will quiet you with his love." Because Sophie was so vulnerable and sensitive, she became easily agitated. But she never failed to become peaceful and relaxed when with her parents.

"He will rejoice over you with singing." The last sentence of the Scripture verse blew my mind when I remembered the songs composed and sung especially for Sophie by her mother.

All my defenses were down. It was all so clear. My flawed condition had not lessened my value in God's eyes; it had not doomed me to eternal displeasure or disapproval. Instead, my flawed condition had served to stir all the resources of faithfulness, self-sacrifice, and love of my Creator.

I could see how logical, right, and good it was for Sophie's parents to pour out their love on their far-from-perfect child, for she was their own flesh and blood, begotten from their own bodies. In loving her, they were loving themselves.

How much more logical, right, and good it now seemed to me for God, my Creator, who made me in His image, to relate to me in a similar way.

DISABILITIES OF BODY, MIND AND SPIRIT

Children like Sophie, with severe disabilities, are often at great risk of being neglected or maltreated when they are born into societies with meager resources, especially where the family unit is not strong. Sophie was unusually fortunate.

It is noteworthy that after her death at age 15, her parents devoted their energies to setting up a facility where children with various disabilities can be given the care and attention they need. They have named it Sophie's Place.

Undoubtedly, we have seen an increasing awareness and concern in the Caribbean region for such children. This is good. There is however a form of disability that is extremely common among our children but often passes unnoticed. It is a disability of the mind and spirit, resulting from the belief that a person is inferior because of skin color or socio-economic background.

Maria was one such child. She tells of the spiritual and emotional breakthrough that she experienced when, as a young Christian, she first understood her dignity and worth in God's eyes:

"I am the child of a racially mixed union. My mother is black. In the Caribbean island where I was born, my father passed for white.

"My mother is a woman with a very engaging personality who has had to work hard all her life in order to survive. She is street smart and tough, and meets the challenges of life with a hearty laugh and a glass of rum. She is not a drunk, but according to local standards she is considered 'common.' I use the term with horror. She became pregnant with me when she was 18 years old.

"My father is of mixed English, Carib Indian, and Jewish origins. He is fair in complexion with straight black hair. His family was far from wealthy, but in a society where blacks are the majority and whites are put on a pedestal, he had the world of women at his feet. I was one in a series of offspring, the fruit of his many romantic escapades.

"When I was 15 months old, I was legally adopted by my father's sister and her husband, an electrical engineer. My new mother left her job at the bank to take care of me. Both Mum and Dad loved me dearly. I was cherished and protected; some say I was pampered and spoilt.

"We did not have everything, but we were comfortable. We traveled abroad. Above all, we moved socially among those who were white, middle class, or upper class.

"My introduction to the wider world came when I entered secondary school. I could have gone to the more elitist convent school, but I chose to attend the school located closer to home. There, for the first time, I rubbed shoulders with so-called working-class children. They were mainly black and poor. It was there that I realized how different I was from the majority of my island peers.

"I am noticeably of African descent. My hair is coarser than that of most black women. My mouth is wide and generous, with full lips, and my complexion is light brown. Yet my schoolmates never accepted me as black or as one of them. I wasn't dark-skinned enough, my house was too big, and my family was mostly white. Daily I suffered at their hands.

"The irony of it was that my mother belonged to the working class. But I had learned early in life to dislike and avoid everything that was true of my mother. I learned that she couldn't be trusted, that she wanted to whisk me away to live with her. The pain I endured from my working-class schoolmates served to confirm my mistrust of her.

"In the end, I totally rejected my blackness and deliberately chose to belong to the white world. I straightened my hair, kept out of direct sunlight as much as possible, and sought the company of those accepted as white, all the while hating my Negroid features with every fibre of my being. Bitterly, I railed at God's "injustice" in making me the only one in my father's family who was noticeably black.

"I lived a double life. On the outside, I was proper and well-spoken, performing like an actor permanently on stage. On the inside, I was tormented by deep feelings of self-hatred and loathing for those blacks who rejected me. I deeply desired to be white. At the same time, I envied those who appeared free to be themselves. It was while in this state of denial and hypocrisy that I met Faith Linton.

"I was an 18-year-old student at the time, a born-again Christian attending the Discipleship Training School of Youth With A Mission in St. Croix, Virgin Islands. During my time there, on December 22, 1992, God spoke to me through prophecy. The message revealed that God was calling me to serve Him in the Caribbean region. He wanted to use me to help bring healing to black people as they found their identity in Jesus Christ.

"I rejected the call and put the message out of my mind. Given my background and the many hurts I had suffered, the message seemed completely incongruous.

"In January 1993, our DTS group visited Jamaica. There Faith spoke to us about the history and culture of the African-Caribbean people. My eyes were opened and I recognized the lies of slavery that we had embraced. I realized that the identity crisis and the hypocrisy that I saw in black people were realities—not figments of my imagination.

"Then Faith taught us who we were in God's eyes, according to Genesis 1 and 2. A powerful word. For the first time, I appreciated the dignity we have as human beings, black as well as white, because we were all made in the image of God.

"I remember that day as if it were yesterday. Then and there, healing began to take place in my life. I remember leaving the room after that session with a sense of deep joy. For the first time in my life I was proud to be black and told God with great exuberance that I was happy that He had made me black.

"It was there that I forgave all the black people who had rejected me. This radical change in my attitude towards myself and issues of race, color, and class led to the healing of my relationship with my biological mother and adoptive mother. Moreover, the seed was planted that has become a major goal of my life: to see my own people set free from the mental chains of slavery, embracing God's love and the dignity of their creation in His image, and accomplishing His purpose, individually, culturally, and nationally.

"On March 3, 1993, as I was preparing to leave St. Croix to return home, someone handed me the tape of the prophecy that I had rejected. As I listened to it, I wept. As the Holy Spirit confirmed the prophecy to me, I was able to receive it. At last I could understand the reason why God made me black in a majority white family. Through that experience, He prepared me for the ministry to which He has called me.

"I still had many struggles to go through. As each lie surfaced from deep within my psyche I faced it with God's truth. My hair and my motives for straightening it are the most recent issue with which I have struggled. The straightened locks have now been cut off and a strong 'afro' has taken their place. I will learn to appreciate and care for this wild, beautiful hair that God has given me.

"I have other responsibilities and greater blessings. Now that I have married my Negro man, we have two wonderful children, our son, Pedayah (God my Redeemer), age 4 years, and our daughter, Abigail (Joy of the Father), age 5 months. We will teach them all that we have learnt: we are created in the image of God, awesomely and wonderfully made. To God we give glory and praise."

EIGHT

WORTH DYING FOR

EIGHT

THERE WERE OTHER EXCITING DEVELOPMENTS FROM THE NEW PERSPECTIVE that the first two chapters of the Bible opened up for me. The most important of these concerned the meaning of the cross.

When I was a student in England, in the 1950s, the evangelical movement was flourishing there. During my first term at University College London (UCL), I started attending the weekly meetings of the London Inter-Faculty Christian Union (LIFCU), an evangelical, inter-denominational student organization.

The members of this organization attracted me by the purity and integrity of their lives and their vibrant faith. I joined them as they met in small groups to pray and study the Bible, and I marvelled. They seemed to be able to relate to God in a direct and personal way. The Bible came alive as we studied together. We sat under the teaching of outstanding men of God, such as Martyn Lloyd-Jones and John Stott, and experienced the power of truth to penetrate our minds and transform our lives in a revolutionary way.

During my first term at UCL, the theme of all the LIFCU meetings was the cross, presented each week from a different perspective. We saw how the cross revealed the attributes of God's character. The cross provided the answer to humanity's dilemma while fully meeting the demands of God's justice and the dictates of His love.

That series of messages gave me a thorough, in-depth understanding of the central truths of the Christian faith. It was a most satisfying and enlightening period in my life. Wherever I went in British evangelical circles, teachers and preachers emphasized the centrality and significance of the cross. Basic to this teaching was the fact of the utter helplessness and hopelessness of humankind in their sin. Great emphasis was placed on this, for it was sin that had made the cross necessary. The cross was God's answer to the terrible problem of sin. My experience as a Christian during the following 50 years has reinforced this teaching.

However, looking back, I recognize that the profile that was given of humanity was almost completely dominated by its sinful condition. Reference was made to our having been created by God, created to know, love, and serve Him, but these references served mainly to introduce the subject of sinful humanity. They would come under the heading of how sin first came into the world, not under the heading of how humanity first came into the world.

Very little time was spent on what happened before the Fall. There was no detailed exegesis of Genesis 1:26-27 or Genesis 2. There was little or no emphasis on the truth of our original pristine condition. Indeed the word *original* was almost always used in connection with sin, as if our spiritual history were rooted not in the divine image but in sin.

The preacher's priority seemed to be the discussion of the subject of humanity's sinfulness. He seemed to find it unnecessary to spend time portraying human beings as originally conceived in the mind of God. As a result, the fundamental question "Who am I?" was answered in a distorted way, with sin becoming the defining factor.

The irony of it all was that in bypassing the definition of humanity found in Genesis 1 and 2, the preacher missed the one factor essential for convicting us of the seriousness of sin and also for motivating us to seek complete deliverance from this evil.

Look at it this way: if I see myself as an outsider, however grateful I may be for my adoption into God's family I will never have the confidence or motivation necessary for living up to this privilege. On the other hand, a tremendous release takes place within me when my eyes are opened to the fact that God's royal family is where I really belong. I was originally made for the palace; I was originally conceived in the heart and mind of the King.

This realization has changed my whole perspective. I understand and see myself in a totally new way. I therefore reject all that debases me and wholeheartedly embrace the God-image that Christ offers to restore in me.

This realization added a new dimension to the meaning of the cross. God's astounding offer of grace through the cross reveals not only His compassion and mercy but also the enormous value He places on me as a human being made in His image. Everything fell into place when I saw this.

Before, I had always puzzled over the obvious unworthiness of humankind as the object of God's extraordinary act of self-giving on the cross. Why would God extend Himself in such an unbelievable way on behalf of such unworthy creatures?

Genesis 1 and 2 provided the answer. It was humankind's value and worth in God's eyes that made sense of God's action in sacrificing His only Son for our sake. That was what justified the incredible price He was prepared to pay for restoring us to Himself. The fact is, we are worth dying for.

I became aware that Jesus emphasized our value and worth in His teachings. Passages of Scripture that I had known for decades suddenly opened up, shedding new light on how God perceived me. When Jesus debated with the Jews in favor of healing a man's shrivelled hand on the Sabbath, his main point was the value of the human being (Matthew 12:9-13). When He sought to persuade His followers to stop being anxious and worried, His main argument was founded on our value in God's eyes (Matthew 6:25-27; Luke 12:22-24).

When I read Matthew 16:26 I caught a glimpse of my immense worth, for the value of the whole world cannot compare with my value as a living soul.

This discovery of who I really am delivered me from a kind of skepticism towards God's promises in Christ. On the one hand, I yearned to enter the unsearchable riches of Christ. On the other hand, it all seemed unattainable, too good to be true—until my eyes were opened to passages such as Ephesians 1 and 1 John 3:1-2.

These passages were not new to me, but something had blocked my understanding of them. I was locked into a debased perception of who I was. Therefore, my response to the truths found in these passages was influenced by this distorted self-concept. Ephesians 1 showed me how wrong my thinking was. My destiny as a child of God and joint heir with Christ had been predetermined, decided before my existence, even before the creation of the world. This meant that the Creator designed me with a purpose in mind. He made me for life in the heavenly royal family, not for the junkyard.

It was a major breakthrough! I now saw the beauty and holiness of the Son of God, which had always seemed to me unattainable, as the spiritual state and condition for which I had been created. Holiness, not sinfulness, was the norm, the truly natural condition. God in Christ was not trying to make a silk purse out of a sow's ear. He was restoring the torn and tattered silk purse to its original beauty and perfection. Seeing my value in this way made a world of difference.

Now I can better appreciate all that is implied in the words of the apostle John when he wrote: "How great is the love the Father has lavished on us, that we should be called children of God! And that is what we are!" (1 John 3:1). I used to understand this statement to mean that God was only able to lavish His love on me and see me as His child after Jesus died for me. Now I know that God's love was not an afterthought resulting from pity at our depraved condition. As the apostle Paul wrote in Ephesians 1:4-5, before the world was created, God predestined us, in love, to be adopted as His children through Jesus Christ.

From the very beginning, God lavished His love on me when He chose to make me in His image. From eternity, He resolved to create beings worthy of His love, privileged beings on whom He would bestow the highest honor accorded any living creature, that is, to be like Him. Being in His image is the precondition to our being adopted as His sons and daughters through Jesus Christ.

Sin presented an awesome challenge to the love of God. His response to that challenge has given us overwhelming proof of how greatly He loves us. But our greatest experience of His love is yet to come. The love supremely manifested on the cross will be fully understood and experienced by us only when we have become wholly like Him and see Him as He is. As the apostle John points out: "Dear friends, now we are children of God, and what we will be has not yet been made known. But we know that when he appears, we shall be like him, for we shall see him as he is" (1 John 3:2). When I saw this, John's concluding statement attracted, stirred, and motivated me as never before: "Everyone who has this hope in him purifies himself, just as he is pure" (1 John 3:3).

NINE

FATHER HUNGER APPEASED

IT IS AUGUST 12, 2003, THE FIRST NIGHT OF THE INTER SCHOOL CHRISTIAN Fellowship (ISCF) discipleship camp held at Moorlands, in the cool hills above the town of Mandeville, Jamaica. Fifty youngsters, age eleven to seventeen years, have come together here from all over the island. It is 10:00 p.m., and in each of the dorms seven or eight campers are gathered around their counselors for dorm devotions. They all have some knowledge of God, Jesus, and the Bible, and most of them say they are Christians. They are quiet and attentive as the dorm leader asks this surprising question: "Suppose you were to die tonight and find yourself at the Gates of Heaven. The gatekeeper meets you and asks: 'What good reason can you give me for allowing you to enter Heaven?' What would you say?"

The answers are disturbing, but predictable. Ninety percent of the campers say something like this: "I go to church, read my Bible, pray, and am trying to be a good Christian." Only a small minority affirm that their hope of Heaven rests entirely on the finished work of Jesus, the Son of God.

Later, as the camp proceeds, another doctrinal aberration comes to light. Several of the campers believe that if they were to die suddenly without having had the chance to confess their most recently committed sins, they would go to Hell, even though they profess to be Christians who have put their trust in the Lord Jesus.

Clearly, these campers had little or no understanding of God's grace; that is, the free, generous gift of a compassionate God to us, His created beings, when we least deserved it. The camp leadership faced a major challenge. Where were these ideas coming from? How should we deal with these campers and their needs?

As a Bible study leader, I needed to have answers to these questions. It was not enough for me to have an understanding of the teaching of Scripture, essential as that was. I needed to know who these youngsters were, the circumstances that had shaped their self-concepts, the experiences that were influencing their views of God and authority figures in general, and in particular, what made them so vulnerable to the kind of distorted ideas they were being taught about God and salvation.

FAMILY BREAKDOWN

Out of my childhood experience in rural Jamaica, as well as my subsequent experience as a high school teacher and camp counselor, I was convinced that many of the answers we sought were rooted in generations of a broken, dysfunctional pattern of family life. Paternal deprivation is the rule rather than the exception in our society. Even where the father is present in the home, his role and relationship with his children are often limited to providing financial support and administering punishment.

In the majority of homes, the stable figure is the mother or grandmother. She nurtures, disciplines, and provides for the children. She holds things together. The adult males tend to come and go. In some cases there is literally a succession of different men coming and going over a period of time. These men may or may not be able to find a job, and when they do, providing for home and children may not be top priority. Too often they are perceived as irresponsible, unreliable, and self-centered.

The men and women of our society have hopes and expectations of each other similar to those of people all over the world. But they often become disillusioned and frustrated with each other, which sometimes leads to abuse and violence. The children have a hard time. In general, parents tend to be punitive and abusive in raising their children. When the relationship between the parents breaks down, the children suffer even more. The over-burdened single mother, for example, may use threats, blows, and curses in an effort to control her children. She may release her feelings of anger and frustration with her man onto her children. Usually, she finds the teenage boys most difficult to manage. In desperation she will tell them: "You worthless good-for-nothing. You will never come to anything—just like your worthless father."

It is no wonder that some of our youngsters have a warped idea of God. I remember leading a session that dealt with the topic "The Father-heart of God." During the discussion time, a young woman, attractive, intelligent, and articulate, got up and said, "I am a Christian, but I can't call God Father because the word father...." She did not finish the sentence, but the look on her face and the gesture she made with her hand expressed her disappointment and disgust.

How alarming that such a negative reaction to the word *father* should have persisted well after this young woman's conversion and continued to influence her attitude to God. It is no coincidence that *father* describes both our human parent and God. Our experience with the former was obviously meant to prepare us for our relationship with our Creator. In the Jamaican situation, where fathering has, in many cases, broken down so badly, we need to take into account the fact that this breakdown can and does affect the way we preach and teach about God and the way Jamaicans react to the gospel.

A Distorted View of the Father

When a preacher talks about God as Father, what picture of God does he convey, and what picture comes to the mind of his hearers? Biblically, the word *father* is meant to evoke a sense of trust, warmth, security, and joyful anticipation. How many Jamaican children respond that way? How many preachers can, out of their own childhood experience, flesh out the image of God in these terms?

How many, without realizing it, project onto God the distorted impressions they have received from their experiences with their own human father? Consider for example, the common Jamaican stereotype of a good father as one who is a stern, harsh disciplinarian and who instills fear in the hearts of his children, teaching them right from wrong mainly by administering severe corporal punishment. One would have expected the church to make a conscious effort to counteract the influence of this stereotype and to present a more balanced picture of God based on the Scriptures. Instead, too often we hear from evangelists, especially, a view of God in which the emphasis is heavily on anger, punishment, and judgment.

No wonder one young man pictured God as a great, big Being who kept shaking His head in disapproval as He looked down on him. No wonder so many accept teaching that makes God out to be first and foremost a Judge who requires confession of every single misdeed before He will pardon and accept the Christian, for whom Jesus died, into Heaven.

Clearly, fear motivates these Christians to do what God requires, just as it is for many Jamaican children in relation to their human fathers. Nothing in such a child's experience has prepared her for a Father who wants, above all, a close, loving relationship with His children. She knows nothing of the powerful bond created by acceptance, approval, and a sense of belonging. She is not motivated to identify with the Beloved, wanting to be like Him and to please Him above all else.

Instead she lives in a state of anxiety as she undertakes the responsibility of qualifying herself for entry to Heaven. For her, the emphasis is not relationship but survival, that is, making it out of Hell and into Heaven.

Here again, one would have expected the church to make a special effort to minister to such people, bringing them the amazing news of God's grace. They would learn of the perfect and complete provision made in Christ for meeting all the requirements that they could not meet themselves. They would discover that this provision includes both the forgiveness of sins and the gift of righteousness. They would recognize that by this provision God removes all barriers to intimacy with Himself, which is His main desire.

Instead, one hears reports of pastors deliberately withholding from their congregations the truth about a free and full salvation. They are afraid that their church members, having lost all fear of death, punishment, and Hell, will throw off all restraint and start sinning without compunction. What an astounding admission of mistrust of God's wisdom and integrity and the efficacy of the work of Christ. How could one imagine that the very plan of God to deal with sin would be so flawed that it would give the sinner greater freedom to sin? Surely the opposite must be the case. Surely the sinner, who enters into the complete and perfect provision made by Christ, is both motivated and empowered to love and serve God with all his heart. There is plenty of evidence to support this.

Reference has already been made to the fact that historically the breakdown of the Jamaican family, and in particular the role of the father, dates back to the days of slavery in the Caribbean, between the 16th and 19th centuries. As we have already seen, Jamaicans, most of whom are descendants of African slaves, continue to experience the effects of this period in our history. We feel these effects in virtually every area of our lives: spiritual; emotional; psychological; relationships with God, family, friends and acquaintances; and concept of self.

Take the matter of self-concept. The stigma attached to slavery still influences the way we see ourselves. It manifests itself, for example, in the dangerous practice of bleaching the skin to make the color more brown, less black. Parents speak disparagingly of the child whom they describe as "black 'n ugly like a monkey." Skin color has traditionally been linked with educational achievement and moral integrity. In a rural Jamaican market in the 1960s, a black saleswoman made this comment about a brown-skinned customer: "When you see them that color, you can trust them."

Family dysfunction only serves to perpetuate and deepen the poor self-concept of the black child. When a child experiences neglect, deprivation, or abuse from his parents, he receives a strong, clear message about himself. He concludes that he is not worthy of his parents' constant presence, love, and care; he does not deserve their time and attention. Worse, he may conclude that he deserves pain and punishment. The child perceives that his parents disapprove of him, even reject him. And he is likely to conclude that God's attitude to him must be similar to that of his parents.

The child goes to school and encounters teachers who reinforce the message of disapproval, for teachers often follow the patterns of child-rearing practised at home. Saddest of all, when the child goes to church, the evangelist, beginning his message at Genesis chapter 3, confirms what parents and teachers have already inculcated. He is a wretched, helpless sinner, deserving God's wrath and judgment. True as this may be, when this truth is taught outside the context of our original creation in God's image, the effect can be totally misleading. This is especially likely to happen if our earliest experiences have already convinced us that we have little value or significance.

Such a child is particularly vulnerable to a kind of religion that is highly legalistic, because of his deep need to prove his worth and significance. The mind of the legalistic Christian is preoccupied with questions such as: How do I compare with the person next to me? Do others see me as a good Christian?

Because his legalism is rooted in low self-esteem, he is plagued with anxiety and envy if he perceives the other person to be doing better than himself. His self-hatred makes honest self-appraisal difficult, if not impossible. He dares not face up to the truth about himself, because he dares not discover how often he fails. Therefore, he frequently lives in denial and self-deception and is hypersensitive to any suggestion of criticism or disrespect from others.

He balks at the idea of grace, because grace gives him no opportunity to prove himself, to demonstrate his worth and significance, and he is desperate to be able to do so. Moreover, because he is unaware of his spiritual identity and his value in God's eyes, he finds it hard to reconcile the amazing generosity of God with his own unworthiness. Somehow it does not seem right that God should set him free from all his obligations. He cannot accept grace; he must first of all feel worthy.

The only cure for the legalistic Christian is a strong dose of Genesis 1 and 2. When this teaching is effectively applied, it does away with the need for him to prove himself. It lays the foundation of his significance and value in God's eyes, establishes his identity, and tells him where he really belongs. It gives the rationale for God's grace. For sin has not diminished his worth and value; therefore, unworthy sinner though he may be, in God's eyes he is worth dying for.

The descendants of slaves and the products of dysfunctional homes discover through Genesis 1 and 2 that no disadvantage—race, class, poverty, lack of education, neglect, deprivation, or abuse—can disqualify them from the heritage for which they were originally created. It is this heritage that Jesus can restore to them by grace.

LEGALISM VERSUS RELATIONSHIP

Unfortunately, legalism makes a good impression in some church circles. We do not always recognize that legalistic Christians are seeking to create their own righteousness, a completely useless exercise, as Paul explains in the letter to the Romans (10:3-4). Legalism was the religion of the scribes and Pharisees, which Jesus so strongly condemned in Matthew 5-7. In this passage, the Sermon on the Mount, Jesus pointed out that the righteousness that God requires is of a higher quality and different kind than the righteousness we can achieve through keeping rules and regulations and achieving human-made goals. That is why only Jesus could provide this kind of righteousness, which we receive as a gift, by faith (Romans 3:21-22).

This important aspect of Christ's work, this crucial part of Christ's complete provision for our salvation and our reconciliation with God, is not always emphasized and highlighted as it ought to be; hence the prevalence of legalism.

What makes legalism totally unacceptable is the fact that it blocks and hinders our relationship with God. The legalistic spirit engenders pride in our achievements, which runs counter to the biblical requirement of a humble, repentant heart in those who draw near to God.

Humility and repentance necessitate self-knowledge—an honest facing-up to the truth about ourselves. The legalistic Christian resists this kind of honesty because the truth would be too shattering to his already low self-esteem. Only those who are fully and deeply conscious of their value and significance to God, those who are secure in Christ's complete provision of forgiveness and righteousness, are free to recognize and acknowledge the depths of their sinfulness.

True humility and repentance are the work of the Holy Spirit. It takes time. He works in us so that we increasingly see ourselves as God sees us and want for ourselves what God wants for us. We learn to see both our original value and worth and our present depraved condition, and we increasingly desire that the image of God be restored in us.

If I am anxiously preoccupied with the legalistic necessity of maintaining an all-encompassing and up-to-date confession of my sin, I tend to be turned in on myself. I therefore fail to be attentive to the gentle probing of God's Spirit as He patiently and lovingly enables me to admit to and turn away from all that separates me from God and to apply myself to building my relationship with God. This is the Spirit's work, not mine; but I need to be attentive and responsive to Him. If I am not preoccupied with earning my way into Heaven, and if I am assured that Jesus has done all that is necessary on my behalf, then I can turn all my energies to the wonderfully rewarding task of learning to know, to please, and to enjoy God. This was what the youngsters at ISCF Discipleship Camp 2003 needed to know.

How could we help them enter into these truths? We depended mainly on the daily Bible study series. First, we sought to establish the greatness, character, power, and sovereign rule of God. Then, we highlighted the worth and dignity of human beings, created in the image of God and intrinsically valuable in God's eyes. Against this background, humanity's fall into sinfulness was presented as a tragic situation crying out for redemption, a God-size problem to which God's response was one of self-sacrificial love and amazing grace. His was a logical response, for it would be unthinkable for God to permit the enemy to defeat His original purpose for humanity, unthinkable that He should turn His back on those in whom he had invested so much—His very image. No cost was too great to pay for the restoration of His masterpiece, humanity, the pinnacle of His creation.

As the camp proceeded, it was heartwarming to hear the responses and the prayers of the campers. Some were moved to tears as they prayed. They voiced their enthusiasm and awe at the greatness of God, their new-found dignity and appreciation of themselves as God's masterpiece, their relief at the God-size solution to the God-size sin problem, and their wonder and joy at the grace and love of God.

This was of God, and we were thankful. God was answering our prayers. The campers had recognized the close connection between humans and God. We believe that out of this awareness, a relationship with God as Father would follow.

Then I asked them: "Suppose your mother found this poem among the books and papers in your room, one day while you were away at school. What would she say to you when you returned home?" Several of the group responded to my question, and every answer was negative: their mothers would have been shocked, angry, or concerned.

When I disclosed where I had taken it from, they were speechless. They had obviously expected me to agree with their mothers and, in the name of Christianity, warn them about the temptations of the flesh. That quotation from the Bible just did not fit into their understanding of sexual purity. Surely God was too holy to contemplate, much less be held responsible for, that kind of behaviour.

Undoubtedly, many generations of Christian young people, dating back, some say, to St. Augustine of Hippo, have been fed negative teaching on human sexuality. Many evangelical Christian women in the early 20th century sincerely believed it was wrong for a Christian woman to enjoy sexual intercourse.

But a change is taking place. For example, over the past 50 years a great deal of literature has been published that provides information and a more balanced, positive view of human sexuality. Above all, the biblical view of sex has been well researched and promoted.

Despite all this, here in Jamaica, change to a more positive, wholesome view of sex has been slow. We are still at the stage where we are uncovering the range and extent of the damage experienced by young and old as a result of continuing dysfunctional sexual behaviour. This includes rape, incest, promiscuity, and sexual abuse of minors, with their attendant evils, such as a high incidence of sexually transmitted disease. In addition, there is the mental and emotional trauma, which can affect the victim's life in various and lasting ways.

These problems are also increasing in countries such as the UK and the USA. This, in turn, is having an impact on the situation in the Caribbean, since we are strongly influenced by the North American culture in religious, social, cultural, and economic matters. At the same time, we need to remember that the Afro-Caribbean people have had a very different historical experience from North Americans of Caucasian origin.

In family life matters, for example, up until the 1950s, marriage was the norm in virtually all First World countries. This was not so among the African Diaspora in the West. Beginning in the 16th century, when the slave trade brought thousands of Africans to the West, a brutal and deliberate destruction of family ties and relationships took place among them. Not even the influence of Christianity in the last 200 years has succeeded in restoring to the Afro-Caribbean people the elements of stable family life.

Indeed, there are deep-seated attitudes among our young people that can be traced back to the days of slavery. Deprived of the right to maintain their traditional, stable African family lifestyle, the slaves were exposed instead to sexual exploitation by their morally degenerate slave masters. It included the ravishing of the female slaves, sadism, sexual torture, and the rape of infant slaves.

Evidence of the continuing influence of this era has surfaced in recent times. During the course of a research project carried out in Jamaica in the 1990s, the following conversation took place between the researchers and males at a prominent high school that participated in the project:

Researchers:	"Is sex pleasurable?"
Males:	"Oh, yes!"
Researchers:	"Pleasurable for whom?"
Males:	"For the man, of course."
Researchers:	"What about the woman?"
Males:	"Women must suffer, they must feel pain."

The question arises: Why has the church been ineffective in changing these grossly distorted and damaging attitudes and ideas? Let us remember that the British missionaries who evangelized our African slave ancestors were products of the Victorian era, and therefore inadequately equipped to tackle the appallingly depraved situation in Jamaica.

They were certainly not strangers to sexual immorality. It was common knowledge that many respectable Victorian men lived a double life. On the one hand, they would uphold Christian standards as head of a household appropriate to their station in life. At the same time, they might also be discreetly maintaining a mistress and offspring in a second household.

However the blatant disregard for propriety among the white slave masters and their almost total lack of decency and humanity in sexual matters was depravity beyond the Victorian missionaries' experience.

It is unlikely that they understood the deep severity of the problem. They could hardly have foreseen the far-reaching results of the slave masters' actions, how generations to come would suffer because male slaves were deprived of their right to live with their wives and relate closely to their children. The role of the committed husband and father has been lost. We struggle even now to restore it.

Still the question remains: Is the gospel limited in its power to transform society? Are there certain situations that are beyond its power? Surely not. The gospel is not limited. Human beings are. And sometimes we impose limitations on the gospel that render it ineffective in certain situations.

For example, the Victorian preacher considered it inappropriate, even offensive, to deal with certain personal matters in public. But these personal matters were precisely what needed to be addressed in Caribbean slave society. Such was the sexual degradation, the moral and emotional trauma, to which the slaves had been subjected that it was not enough to teach the eager new converts the Ten Commandments and the tenets of the moral law. Their condition required deep emotional and spiritual therapy.

Sexual abuse and degradation leads to a low sense of self-worth, which affects every aspect of a person's being. We lose our identity as valuable people and tend to treat others as non-persons. When sexual degradation is linked with other oppressive and dehumanizing conditions of slavery, the effects are bound to be deeply damaging. Therefore, the slaves needed a well-informed, aggressive program of teaching and ministry designed to root out the demons of self-hatred, hopelessness, purposelessness, and alienation. Specifically they needed to rediscover that sex was designed by God to be wholesome and good. The pleasure and satisfaction we can experience in sex are God's gifts to us, made possible by the way He created our bodies. Moreover, two people in an exclusive, lasting relationship can find the fullest expression of intimacy, trust, and their commitment to each other in sexual union. These are the truths that such a program would seek to restore.

We need that program even more now. At the heart of such a program must be the biblical teaching of the human being's creation in the image of God. It is first of all in Genesis 1 and 2 that we discover our identity, meaning, and significance as persons. According to those two chapters, persons are sexual beings; that is, we come in two kinds, male and female. As male and female in God's image we represent different aspects of God's personality, the masculine aspect and the feminine. Above all, we express the complete image of God when man and woman unite and become one in a lifelong exclusive relationship, because relationship is the ultimate expression of the image of God.

ELEVEN

TWO WORLDS, TWO FRIENDS

As I look back over the past 70 years, I can trace the remarkable way that God has directed and overruled the circumstances of my life in order to bring health and wholeness to my damaged psyche, as He worked patiently to restore His image in me.

I marvel above all at the persons He placed in my life. The older I grow the more thankful and appreciative I feel towards my parents, teachers, spiritual leaders, and mentors. They were, for the most part, persons of character, principled, and godly, chosen to influence me in the formative years. I have also been specially blessed in my friends. Of these there are two whose impact on my personal development I cannot measure: my husband, Ivan, and my "soul sister," Lucy.

When Ivan first came into my life he was a 20-year-old Jamaican student in England, like me. Though we had both attended high school in the same town, we had never met until we went to London, where we found ourselves attending Westminster Chapel.

Undoubtedly, we had a great deal in common. At the same time, our life stories differed in crucial ways. Ivan was a farmer's son; my parents were schoolteachers. As a boy, he was free to roam the fields and bushes, rose early to milk the cows, heard the birdcalls and knew each bird by name. His mother loved gardening, and he became her eager assistant. Effortlessly, he absorbed knowledge of flowers, plants, trees, crops, and animals. They were all part of his daily life and duties, part of his family heritage and his parents' world.

By contrast, being a girl, I was sheltered and protected. My duties kept me mainly indoors. Though my father loved the land and farmed his few acres with pride and joy, farming was his hobby. Teaching was his life. A bookworm and a thinker, he delighted in discussing politics and the problems of the society with his friends. So the world of books and issues became mine, too.

Ivan's mother, affectionately called Miss Leety, lived a busy life. She had eight children. In addition, following a pattern common in Jamaica then, a succession of other people's children joined the family from time to time. While Ivan's father worked on the farm, Leety ran the family business, a shop stocked with grocery and hardware items, tools, animal feed, and the daily newspaper. Out in front of the shop stood a petrol pump. In an old-fashioned brick oven, seven feet high, Miss Leety would bake bread, bulla, and buns for sale in the shop. She also took orders for wedding cakes. And when she could sit for a while, she sewed dresses on her sewing machine, conveniently set up in the shop, while the newest baby slept peacefully in a homemade "cradle" under the shop counter.

Bustle and activity, the unpredictable and the unexpected—that became Ivan's idea of life; and he loved it that way.

On the other hand, my parents had only three children, my twin sister, brother, and myself. Peace and quiet reigned, sometimes to the point of boredom, in our little wooden cottage tucked away in a secluded corner of the lush countryside in the hilly interior of the island.

There were always folk coming and going in Ivan's home, which stood on the edge of a busy main road. For me, visitors were a rare and special treat.

Our household was ruled by the bell. It was a brass hand bell, and it stood on my father's desk on a platform at one end of the wooden schoolhouse where he was head teacher. He rang it at 9:00 a.m. for school-call, at noon for lunchtime, mid-morning and mid-afternoon for recess, and at 4:00 p.m., the ending of the school day. My sister and I imbibed order and a structured way of life with our mother's milk, literally. Mama went back to her teaching job when her babies were three months old. Fortunately, the school was only a stone's throw away from the teachers' cottage, so she was able to continue breast-feeding us by coming home at lunch and recess times, according to the bell. Later, the experience of six years of boarding school only served to establish and strengthen my perception that the world was a structured, orderly place.

So when Ivan and I joined our lives in marriage, the biggest challenge was lifestyle. The process of adjustment was traumatic at times. Change was inevitable. Even in the midst of the trauma, I recognized how salutary the process was for me. I needed someone to help deliver me from an unrealistic perfectionism, from too rigid an expectation that law and order must always prevail. Ivan, sanguine, flexible, pragmatic, optimistic, was just what was needed.

More than anything else, I needed to be delivered from the way I perceived myself in relation to other people. I tended to see people in categories according to color, class, education, and culture. Based on what I had learnt in boarding school, culture meant things like the way a person spoke and social skills, including niceties such as the correct use of the spoon, the tip for porridge, the side for soup. According to my way of perceiving people, my category determined my value and worth, and therefore how much time and attention I deserved from those in a superior category. Life with Ivan blew that perception apart, especially by the way he related to those less fortunate than himself.

To him, some persons may have been less fortunate, but that did not make them one whit less important than himself or any other person. Added to that, he could somehow see potential in the most unlikely individual. It became an important part of his mission in life to draw out and nurture that potential in specific persons, usually youths who crossed his path as he moved out into the world of commerce, farming, and horticulture.

The results of his mentoring have been nothing short of amazing. The young men whose need for employment and personal and spiritual development first drew his attention in the 1960s still, 40 years later, express their gratitude to him. They still look up to him as a father figure. In a few cases, they have become part of our extended family. Modelling themselves after Ivan, they have developed positive work habits and have been able to move out of economic and social poverty. Encouraged and even tutored by Ivan, some have improved their literacy and numeracy skills. As a result, they have emerged like the butterflies from their nondescript chrysalises, and their unique gifts and abilities have come to light.

Unlike many of their peers, they have married and in raising their children have shown the same involvement, care, and concern that Ivan showed them in their developing years. Roderick, for example, who grew up fatherless and in abject poverty, failing miserably in school, came to us asking for a job when he was a teenager. Ivan became to him the father he had never known. He is now a married man in his 40s, with four sons, and his wise, attentive parenting together with the close bond between himself and his boys have stirred the admiration of his village. He is also highly regarded there as an enterprising and successful entrepreneur.

Here is a remarkable example of the successful application of the principles of Genesis 1. According to those principles, no one, however deprived or depraved, is beyond hope, beyond remedy. They may suffer great disadvantages because of cultural and educational deficiencies or because of prejudice based on color and class. These disadvantages may indeed hinder their development; they may damage but not destroy the image-of-God material of which they are made. Clearly it was worth all the time and effort Ivan took to salvage and restore those originally made in the image of God.

The book of Genesis, the life and example of my husband, the combined effect of principle and practice, precept and example, radically changed my thinking and attitude.

LUCY

Ivan's role, crucial and all-important as it was, provided only a part of the solution to my distorted perception of people. My friend Lucy provided what was still lacking. I still needed to be cured of my overrated idea of those who seemed to have all the advantages. Lucy was such a person, or so it seemed to me.

She was what we call "Jamaica white." Her family had been landowners on the island for generations but had been careful to keep their racial purity. Under normal circumstances we might never have met each other, since we moved in different social circles. But Lucy was a Christian. When I returned to Jamaica after university in England, I started teaching in the same town where she lived and eventually ended up worshipping in the same church denomination as her.

I got to know her very well. To my surprise, she was not only beautiful in appearance, gracious, and well-bred; she was also open, vulnerable, and shyly aware of her weaknesses and inadequacies. By the time

I had taken her down from my pedestal of perceived racial and social superiority, we had already bonded in one of those friendships that define the meaning of friendship.

Lucy was an excellent listener—empathetic, non-judgmental, keenly interested in the human condition. We talked for hours. At least, I talked and she listened. It all poured out: the internal dissonance and ambivalence created by the two worlds that lived in me, Europe and Africa, with all the social and cultural disparities between the two. I voiced the mistrust, social discomfort, moral unease, lack of emotional and spiritual integrity, and abiding sense of inferiority that resulted from my condition.

Lucy was fascinated. For her it was like seeing her homeland for the first time from an airplane. It gave her a completely new perspective on the ramifications of the society into which she had been born. She was deeply, personally involved in what I was saying, and she listened with all of her being.

For me, this was therapy of the first order. It was not just that I had her full attention. I was being given a sympathetic hearing by a representative from the other side of the fence, as it were. Incredibly, my story made sense to her. More than that, she, like myself, was deeply stirred and radically changed in her perception of the realities of the Jamaican situation by our times of sharing and interaction. I felt vindicated, affirmed. Somehow the two worlds had found a meeting place; they could come to terms and make peace with each other. For me it was a major turning point in my journey towards wholeness.

Clearly, the opening chapters of Genesis provided common ground for my two worlds. I could put into perspective the perceived disadvantages of my race and social class because the truths in these chapters lifted me to unbelievable heights of worth and value. They demonstrate the fallacy of the perception that there are advantages to race and social class that make one person more acceptable to God than another. Indeed, both rich and poor, black and white meet at the same place when we stand before God.

EPILOGUE

"CAN ANYTHING BE MORE WONDERFUL THAN TO SEE LIFE FROM GOD'S POINT of view?" writes Selwyn Hughes.

To see things from God's perspective requires that I change my own perspective on almost everything, beginning with myself. I recognize the lies I have believed, lies such as "You're too ugly; you're a dunce; you're too black, too poor, too lazy."

I have believed my own envious thoughts about my privileged neighbour: "He's superior; I'm inferior. He has everything going for him, good looks, intelligence, education, wealth, and social class. What do I have?"

I may have none of the assets in which so many take pride. Does that make me less a person than the one who is privileged or successful? Certainly not in God's eyes. How does God see me?

He sees His likeness in me and takes delight in it. He values me far beyond my own estimate of my worth.

We simply do not fully grasp what it means to be created in God's image. God first revealed this truth in the Garden of Eden. But we lost its full significance when sin entered the world. It is God's earliest gift to humankind, a gift of love from the riches of His glory.

All persons are of equal importance to God. At the same time, we are all different from each other. Consider this: Since the world began, billions upon billions of people have lived on the earth. Yet each one is unique.

Each time a child is born, God manifests Himself in a new and special way. Because He is infinite, He can never come to an end of new expressions of Himself. Therefore I am unique. There has never been, there is not now and there never will be another person exactly like me. Everyone is indeed made in God's image, but each of us brings something different and special to the complete picture.

At the same time, we face a tragic reality. Sin has distorted God's image in us. Does God grieve? He does, enormously, but He does not despair. He has taken action. Jesus, the Son of God, has already done all that is necessary to restore me, to make me new.

Even now my God and Father rejoices as His Spirit works in me to refashion me, to recreate the image of Jesus in me.

I cannot fully grasp what the finished product will be. It is beyond my imagining. I know enough to catch glimpses of glory, to taste moments of joy. A sure and certain hope grows strongly in my spirit. The future is firmly in God's hands, and it is good.

> The LORD your God is with you,
> he is mighty to save.
> He will take great delight in you,
> he will quiet you with his love,
> he will rejoice over you with singing.
> (Zephaniah 3:17)

CASTLE QUAY BOOKS

For more information and to explore the rest of our titles visit
www.castlequaybooks.com